When I Spoke in Tongues

When
I Spoke
in Tongues

A Story of Faith and Its Loss

❧ JESSICA WILBANKS ❧

BEACON PRESS, BOSTON

BEACON PRESS
Boston, Massachusetts
www.beacon.org

Beacon Press books
are published under the auspices of
the Unitarian Universalist Association of Congregations.

21 20 19 18   8 7 6 5 4 3 2 1

This book is printed on acid-free paper that meets the uncoated paper
ANSI/NISO specifications for permanence as revised in 1992.

Text design and composition by Kim Arney

Some names and other identifying characteristics of people mentioned
in this work have been changed to protect their identities.

Library of Congress Cataloging-in-Publication Data
Names: Wilbanks, Jessica, author.
Title: When I spoke in tongues : a memoir of faith and its loss /
Jessica Wilbanks.
Description: Boston : Beacon Press, 2018.
Identifiers: LCCN 2018008170 (print) | LCCN 2018025549 (ebook) |
ISBN 9780807092248 (ebook) | ISBN 9780807092231 (alk. paper)
Subjects: LCSH: Wilbanks, Jessica | Pentecostal churches—Biography. |
Families—Religious aspects—Pentecostal churches.
Classification: LCC BX8762.Z8 (ebook) | LCC BX8762.Z8 W55 2018 (print) |
DDC 289.9/4092 [B] —dc23
LC record available at https://lccn.loc.gov/2018008170

For my family

I don't believe in God, but I miss Him.

—JULIAN BARNES

Contents

PART I

❦ Chapter 1 ❦

Ghost Language

I moved to Washington at the end of May and by June the humidity snapped shut over the city like a lid. In the mornings steam rose off the sidewalk in long columns, leaving puddles of condensation on the concrete. I had a bright-red Schwinn Classic Cruiser with coaster brakes, and it only took a few minutes of pedaling in that wet heat before my head started pulsing. When I drew a breath, it was as if I was taking in the whole of that city—the rank smell of mulch packed around the flowerbeds, the stench of orange gingko fruit splattered on the sidewalks, the burnt sweetness of restaurant trash piled high in back alleys.

I was twenty-two that summer, freshly graduated from college with a degree in literature, searching for my people. Washington, DC, was just an hour's drive from the rural Maryland town where I grew up, but with the traffic and crowded sidewalks, it felt like another world. I couldn't wait to join the throngs of smartly dressed men and women who packed into the subways every morning, and so I spent most of my time holed up at a coffee shop, emailing my resume out to anyone who might be interested.

3

After a few months, I fell in with a group of activists who congregated a few tables over. They organized weekly protests at the White House and spoke at city council meetings, and afterward they'd meet at Ghana Cafe, a hole in the wall halfway up the hill on Eighteenth Street. One Thursday night over plantains and Star beer, a white woman with tiny, perfect dreadlocks invited me to a meeting in a church basement a few blocks over on Columbia Road. She said they were banding together to fight poverty, homelessness, and inequality, and that sounded good to me.

Of the thirty of us who ended up in that church basement a few nights later, half were religious and the other half were practically minded agnostics who put up with the crucifixes and stained glass because the churches had the meeting space and staff to drive the work forward. So when a balding minister stood in the middle of the room and cleared his throat, asking if we'd join hands for a brief prayer, we all squeezed our eyes closed obediently. He gave a harmless, ecumenical sort of prayer, thanking God, the meeting's cosponsors, and the real estate kingpin who had pledged a thousand dollars to get the coalition going. When the minister gave thanks for the storm that had given us a day's reprieve from the heat we all nodded vigorously, and one woman shouted *amen*.

As the minister's prayer rolled to a close I clasped the bony fingers of the white-haired woman next to me and thought about dinner. But just then a small female voice cut through the minister's baritone. When he paused, that voice became louder and more fervent. I opened my eyes and recognized a Nigerian woman named Beatrice who I had seen at various food drives and fundraisers. She spoke in a raspy

West African cadence blended with clipped British tones, and her words were so thick I had to listen closely to find the English. At times she seemed to be speaking in tongues.

I had picked up bits of Beatrice's story. I knew she was from Nigeria, a country I could pin to a continent but couldn't find on a map. I also knew the vague details of the one great heartbreak of Beatrice's life, a somewhat confusing story she'd tell anyone who'd listen. She had many sons, and most were insolent and lazy, but the youngest one lit up her life. Just before her family left Nigeria, the authorities tested their blood and found that this one good son had a different blood type than the rest of the family. It came out that this boy somehow wasn't her son at all, and that meant when she and her husband and her children came to the United States, that boy had to stay behind.

When Beatrice settled into the grooves of her prayer, she shook her head back and forth in what could have either been praise or fury. *Jehovah! Blessed Jesus! Savior-Lord! King of Kings!* The reds and blues of the stained-glass windows saturated her face as she called out her quarrels with the world. Her back had gone out on her, and her husband had disappeared in a way a man could never disappear in Nigeria—he drove someone to New York City one day and never came back. The woman at the bank called Beatrice daily, threatening to take her house. Her remaining sons had abandoned her for fast-talking girls and nights out with men she didn't know. Beatrice thumped her ribcage with an open palm and just when the minister cleared his throat and inhaled sharply, her tone shifted. She cried out to God again, calling him Father. She told God she loved him, she told Jesus she loved him, and she told the Holy Ghost she loved him.

She said, "I am your servant." She wailed, "Take me into yourself, God! Use me for your will. Wear me like clothes." And then suddenly she went silent, tucking her head and folding her legs demurely. Only a minute or two had passed since she first spoke, and from her posture just then, you'd have thought she never said a word.

While Beatrice prayed, I sat ramrod straight in my chair with a half-smile glued to my face, not trusting myself with the slightest movement. I must have been squeezing the hand of the white-haired woman next to me, because at some point she broke my hold with a dirty look and kneaded the blood back into her fingers. I ignored her and kept my eyes on the minister. In moments of intense emotion, a red flush would bloom over my face and neck, and I was afraid if I so much as glanced in Beatrice's direction, she'd see she had lit a charge under me. She'd know we came from the same people.

Many of the other people in that room called themselves Christians, but they did not believe—as Beatrice did—that the Holy Ghost was a physical presence that could be summoned down from heaven by praying at a great volume. They didn't think of evil as a dark, smoky spirit that could sneak into a person when they turned their back to God, or that bad spirits could be battered out of a person with shouts and oils and fervent prayers. These people were acolytes of Martin Luther King Jr. and Mother Teresa. They wore muted colors, drove sensible ten-year-old cars, and adopted rice-and-bean diets during Lent. They voted for Democrats and believed wholeheartedly in the generically evil forces of poverty and oppression and addiction. If they worshipped God, they left their bodies out of it. They didn't expect the Holy Ghost to open up their hearts or heads and climb inside.

But the God that Beatrice prayed to had been my God once. He was the Alpha and the Omega, the beginning and the end. He was a God known for meddling in the world, rolling his sleeves up and plunging in wrists-deep, unleashing earthquakes and hurricanes to show his displeasure and rewarding his followers with long lives, health, and great riches. That God had allowed the Egyptians to grasp at the hems of the Israelites' robes before releasing the Red Sea at its hinges and washing them away. He helped a boy kill a giant with a slingshot. When his people begged him for a Messiah, a warrior-king who would storm the enemy's gates and rescue his people from oppression, he gave them a baby. That child grew into a man who hung out with a motley crew of tax collectors and prostitutes. Who spoke in slippery stories and never once took up a sword. Who rode to his throne on a donkey and accepted a crown of thorns without as much as a whimper of resistance. Who died on a cross like a common thief before coming to life again. And, in doing so, who healed the world.

His disciples kept his name alive, and two thousand years later, half a billion people had pledged themselves to that particular variety of Jesus. They belonged to various denominations and held slightly different views on water baptism and the rapture, but all followed a strict code of purity and interpreted the Bible's instructions literally. They believed the son of God was born of a virgin, died for our sins, and had been miraculously resurrected on the third day. They believed the world was winding to a close and only the righteous would be saved from hellfire and damnation. They believed God's forgiveness was available to anyone, and all they had to do was believe in God's mercy and repent of their sins. They also believed in the baptism of the Holy Spirit, in which the Holy Spirit burrowed itself into believers, leaving a trail of signs and wonders in its path, turning them into new creatures, releasing them from heathen habits not through their own will, but rather through grace. The outward sign of this state was the gift of tongues—the divinely inspired infusion of a special prayer language that may or may not have a semblance to the languages of this world. I used to speak that language. But that was a long time ago.

When the minister began outlining the goals of the campaign in that church basement on Columbia Road, the elderly woman whose hand I'd been gripping rose from her chair and crouched down next to Beatrice, patting her wrist and talking softly. I could make out snippets of their conversation. The woman knew someone who worked at a credit union who might be able to help Beatrice refinance her house; she also had a nephew who ran in embassy circles and could try to make some headway with the boy. But Beatrice didn't meet her eyes. She just shook her head almost imperceptibly and stared at the floor, her muscles rigid. The white-haired woman paused for a long moment and pursed her lips, then gave Beatrice's hand one final pat and crossed back over to her chair. As she lowered herself down she caught my eye and gave me an expression that said, *Oh well, we tried.*

The minister transcribed the group's ideas on the whiteboard—op-eds and letter-writing campaigns and food pantries. Over time people warmed to the idea of hosting a 5K walk to raise money in the fall, when the weather cleared.

There could be Gatorade stations during it and speeches afterward, and we'd advertise through eye-catching posters. My activist friend offered to get in touch with the designer who had done the images for that anti-malaria campaign. Her dreadlocks bounced as she used her hands to sketch out possible dimensions for the posters. The white-haired woman next to me said she had a route in mind, through Rock Creek Park and ending at the bridge by the zoo.

I stayed quiet. All those phones buzzing on the table intimidated me, as did the way in which the members of the group talked to each other, crossing their arms and interrupting each other and saying just what they meant. I turned slightly and saw that Beatrice was quiet as well, still locked in the same position she'd been in before. A thin band of sweat still haloed her hairline, as if she'd just lifted a heavy boulder. I thought back to the people I'd gone to church with as a child and imagined that if they were here, they'd smile at the idea of fighting poverty through petitions and op-eds and 5K walks. They'd say all that was just sand falling through a fist. They believed in spiritual problems and spiritual solutions. If a city was suffering, then that city needed to humble itself and pray. If someone was hungry, they needed to appeal to the Lord in all his mercy, and he would send help their way. If my old pastor were here, he'd probably be looking at the minister with the same glare that Beatrice was wearing right now, just daring him to throw down his dry-erase marker, fall to his knees, and appeal to that power who was bigger and stronger than any one of us.

I felt an unexpected flush of heat at my neckline again, and when a woman with a blond pageboy wondered out loud how one went about closing the streets for a 5K walk, I surprised myself by cutting in abruptly and leaning forward, telling her in a firm voice that we'd probably need to call the city council and put in a formal request. I told the group that I'd be glad to do it, and then settled into my chair again, arms folded at my chest. The dreadlocked woman winked at me as I took out my notebook to write myself a reminder. The whiteboard listed our next steps in forest green and royal blue and orange and red, and we all packed our things, flush with the possibility of change.

The heat hit me like a wall as soon as I opened the door to Columbia Road. The night before I had seen a television program that argued that the heat was our own fault, that we had done this to ourselves. A professor from some state college in Virginia put on a bowtie for the cameras and told us the more we built up that seventy-mile stretch of swampland at the crook of the Anacostia and the Potomac, the hotter we would get. He said the oaks and poplars in Rock Creek Park were growing eight times faster than trees in Maryland and Virginia; he said the concrete that lined the city absorbed two thousand times more heat than air. He predicted the thunderstorm that would saturate us a few nights later, and he said that when the rainwater evaporated, it would rise up into the clouds for a while and then eventually rain down on us once more.

I tucked my ponytail under my collar, folded my pant leg, and climbed on my bike. My backpack clunked against my spine as I stood up for more leverage, tilting my weight back and forth on the pedals. Part of me enjoyed the pain. I felt the warm wind on my face and didn't mind the calls of the wide-eyed men who ambled around the edges of Malcolm X Park, looking for love or drugs. The world had let them down. They were unwashed and loud and there wouldn't be crowds of well-groomed people surrounding them with reassurances and offers of help, at least not anytime soon. When I was a child, I had been taught that men like these would inherit the earth, that God had blessings in store for them that were greater than any he had for the rest of us, because they were wholly dependent on him. But I didn't believe that anymore. I knew you couldn't wish away pain with prayers. There would be no Messiah coming to comfort the afflicted and set things to rights again.

❧

When I arrived at my brick townhouse on the corner of Mount Pleasant and Park Road, I lugged my fifty-pound bike over my shoulder and unlocked the door one-handed. I'd hoped to see my roommates clustered around our long dining room table sharing a hot meal, but the living room was empty and the dining room table held only a scattered pile of junk mail. Maybe it was just as well. If I tried to tell them about what happened with Beatrice, my elegant roommate Annie would look at me with a quizzical expression and ask me why Beatrice's outburst affected me so much. Drew would run his fingers through his gelled hair and launch into a story about a somewhat unrelated event he'd observed a few months before in the halls of Congress. Jared would be the worst. He'd just gaze at me with his mud-brown eyes and my face would get hot and I'd find myself turning Beatrice into a caricature, just to get a smile out of him.

I heated up a frozen burrito and carried the plate upstairs to my room. It was a relief to close the door on the world. My roommates had become my closest friends, but we had come from different worlds. When they were growing up, their parents cooked French toast on Sunday mornings and traded sections of the *New York Times*. The fact of my Pentecostal upbringing was at best a source of amusement, good for some funny stories after a few bottles of cheap red wine. Once, Annie had asked me if I could still speak in tongues. I denied it, even though part of me wasn't entirely sure.

I first received the gift of tongues when I was eleven years old. One Sunday morning I'd traded my thrift-store dress for a ruffled bathing suit and an extra-large maroon choir robe, and grasped our pastor's hand as he led me down into the chlorinated baptismal font just behind the pulpit. It was the first time I'd been close enough to him to smell his pickled breath or see the dark shadow of his beard underneath his olive skin. I worried about the choir robe, which floated up around me like a cloud and showed my bathing suit, but our pastor probably thought I was having spiritual anxieties and murmured reassuring words.

The pastor placed a calloused hand between the wings of my shoulder blades, and dunked me under the blue-tinged water as I held my nose. My mother and father watched from opposite sides, my father holding his camera at the ready. I knew I should rise up a new creature, but I didn't feel anything shift in the second or two between the dunk and the *whoosh* back to the surface. I just flailed about for a minute, pushing my stringy hair out of my eyes and blindly feeling for the edge of the pool while my mother clutched my bottle-cap glasses, too busy weeping with joy to come to my aid. Beside the pool my father fiddled with his camera angrily, wishing the whole ritual could be done again, and thus documented.

When I realized nothing had changed, a terrible feeling bloomed deep in my belly. But then, a half hour later, pulling my underwear on in the ladies' room, I shivered to myself as I dressed. Out of nowhere my shivers and chatters transformed themselves into strange syllables. There in that bathroom with its pink floral wallpaper, I squeezed my eyes shut and tested my new language, pronouncing those rollicking words slowly at first, and then faster. At some point I lost hold on any one word and slipped into something like song—language that rocked and lurched from one syllable to another. All the power and meaning of any single word melted together into something far greater. Meanwhile I felt like I was lost in a fever dream. I was a shy and awkward kid, but the only thought I had as those unexpected sounds poured out of me was astonishment at my fluency. I didn't bother myself with the meaning of these sounds—that wasn't the point. The point was having this direct line to God, this evidence that the Holy Spirit had entered me and claimed me as his own. Now that same Spirit was reaching back out to God and appealing to him on my behalf.

When the noise trickled to a stop I felt exhausted and wrung out—rinsed clean, the way I sometimes felt after a long crying spell. I opened my eyes and it was as if I was seeing the world for the first time. I was one of God's chosen people. I existed for him alone, to win souls for him and to save people from the Evil One. This was the sign that I had been waiting for. The Holy Ghost was embedded inside me now, and I imagined I'd be different from here on out. Purer in some mysterious way. Lighter, kinder. Less inclined to squabble with my brothers, more likely to help my mother fold laundry or clear the table after dinner. I'd summon up the courage to tell my cousins about what Jesus could do, as they were the only heathens I knew. I'd give my babysitting money to the church. I'd be good, even perfect. I'd finally be worthy.

Back in my room in Washington, my stomach dropped at the memory. These days I didn't believe in the gift of tongues. I explained the phenomenon away as a mass delusion. Anyone could babble nonsense syllables if they found themselves in a situation where that was the expected behavior. I told myself that's what happened to me in that long-ago church bathroom. But that still didn't sit well with me. It didn't explain the thrill of opening my mouth and feeling myself utterly taken over, and then having a language I didn't know come rushing out.

From the window, I watched as the streetlight clicked on, flooding the back alley with fluorescent light, and I started wondering if I could still speak in the tongues of angels. I moved my half-eaten burrito to the side of my desk and tucked my head down and to the right, ever so slightly, closing my eyes and clenching my fists in an effort to call up an entirely different self. Gone was the screen of my laptop, the postcards dotting my robin's-egg-blue walls, my frizzy-haired reflection in the window, and the glow of the streetlight. In the absence of anything visible my thoughts took on a greater weight, and for a while I just watched my anxieties race across the surface of my mind.

After a few minutes, I caught the ragged hook of my breath, smoothing it out and pushing air deep down into my lungs—once, twice, three times, until I felt as empty as an eggshell. I felt my belly begin to roll with the rhythm of those breaths, and then I was eleven again, receiving that heavenly language for the first time. Opening my mouth on faith. Feeling the power of the Spirit pulse through my body. A few syllables came then, springing to my lips with a memorized aspect to them, like remembered phrases from a faraway country I'd visited as a child.

My heart beat faster, and I waited for those syllables to break away into something like a song, but nothing happened. I just kept repeating those same sounds again and again, like a parrot. If there was more of that language in there somewhere, under some layer of subcortical brain matter and sparking electrical pulses, then I didn't know how to reach it. I opened my eyes again and checked my watch. It was just past eight o'clock, and any minute my roommates would trundle in chattering and laughing, with briefcases and grocery bags and bike helmets in hand. If I went downstairs Annie would pour me a glass of cheap cabernet and regale me with stories about her boss, or maybe Jared and I would play a game of Spite and Malice. I knew as soon as I heard the front door creak open I'd cheer up again and push all this business out of my mind.

Scholars of bereavement talk about the damage that results from the loss of the "assumptive world"—the internal framework we use to make sense of our experiences. For me, it wasn't the death of a loved one that rocked me to my foundations, but rather the loss of my faith. It would take ten more years of skirting the margins of the church before I finally started searching for a bridge back to the world I left behind. Eventually my quest to recover my faith would lead me to Beatrice's home country of Nigeria, where I'd attend revivals with hundreds of thousands of people who worshipped God in the same exuberant way I did as a child. I'd travel through the country on *okadas* and *danfos*, collecting stories of miraculous healings and heavenly prophecies from jewel-laden pastors and devoted believers, trying to find a way back into the fold. But all that was still in the future. That night in my room in Washington, all I knew was that I was no longer fluent in the language of the Spirit.

As I waited for my roommates to return home, the minutes ticked by and the house stayed quiet. For a long time I sat there looking out the window with an uneasy feeling, thrumming my fingertips against the edge of my desk and waiting for those empty rooms to fill up with sound.

Chapter 2

House-Hunting

When my family first showed up in southern Maryland in the late eighties, you could drive twenty-five miles on the long, straight highway that cut Calvert County in half and all you'd see would be rolling fields of wet tobacco leaves glittering green in the sun. As the summer wore on, the plants grew as tall as a child and started to flower. In August the pickers would come and move slowly behind the tractors, chopping the stalks close to the root and stacking shiny leaves in heaps, just as they had back when that place was a dead-end town, one of the poorest in Maryland. But times had changed. In the seventies, the nuclear power plant came in, and shortly afterwards a mile-long bridge arced up over the bay and joined the south end of Calvert to the neighboring county. Stoplights followed at Saint Leonard and Lusby and Huntingtown, and then the chain grocery stores put the mom-and-pop shops out of business. Around that time, people from the city started buying land just as fast as the farmers could sell it off. Everywhere you looked it seemed like bulldozers were tearing a hole in the green of the hillside, tracking terra cotta–colored dirt onto the shiny new asphalt highway that had been paid for with tax dollars from the plant.

My father hated those developers with a passion. Burly men in brand-new Ford F150s with sunglasses you couldn't see through and baseball caps with corporate logos, getting rich without getting their fingernails dirty. Shaking your hand with real feeling and then fiddling with their pagers while they sized you up, deciding the encounter wouldn't lead to a sale. My father said they hired boys right out of high school and paid them minimum wage to put up houses from kits with little more than a staple gun and a hammer. He said those houses might look like something from the road, but when you got close you could see them for what they truly were. When you tried to open a door the handle would come off in your hand, and if you tapped the wall hard enough near the baseboard your foot was likely go straight through.

My father was a bricklayer and came up the old way, through a long apprenticeship. But he wouldn't take orders from anyone and didn't believe in punching time cards, so instead he hopscotched from one job to the next, unlicensed and uninsured. Just him and a dusty canvas bag of trowels and his ancient Ford pickup with piles of bricks and mortar pans and bags of sand jumbled up together in the rusted-out bed. Every morning he drove an hour and a half to Old Town Alexandria, where people had the money to pay craftsman's wages for brickwork. When he took out money for materials, a retaining wall or a couple of chimney re-pairs could pay the rent for a month, but sometimes clients were hard to come by. And there were three of us kids to feed, and shoes and underwear to buy, and the pickup truck always needed an alternator or a fan belt, and bricklayers couldn't work in the rain.

We first moved to one of those newfangled houses when our landlord changed his plans on us, deciding to sell the farmhouse we'd been renting just as we were about to renew the lease. We had just thirty days to find a new place, and to my father's dismay, the only house in Calvert County that we could afford was a three-bedroom ranch-style tract house in a development called Nostalgia. The house was just over a thousand square feet with a grey roof and black plastic shutters glued in an open position around the windows in the front of the house. It looked just like the other fifty houses in the neighborhood, only it was white and most of the others were blue or beige or brown.

When the realtor first walked us through that house she talked up the central air and the carpeting and the dishwasher, but that got her nowhere. When my father was a kid in Washington State, he rose two or three times a night to load logs on the woodstove and check the vents, so he thought it was good for my brothers—Obere and Sam—and me to wash the dishes by hand and keep the wood box full. And he didn't approve of the extra expense, even when we didn't turn on the air and just used the fans. When the electricity bill came my father would be in a sour mood for days, and since he didn't have any land to pace he just sat with his arms crossed on the couch, glaring as my mother folded diapers and tried to shush the boys.

Every day we did our best to stay faithful, holding strong in the midst of our trials. For the most part God answered. My uncle Rod came knocking with a doe he'd just killed in the back of his truck, saying his freezer was full and we'd be helping him out if we took her off his hands. We found boys' size eight and size ten sneakers at the same garage sale, just as my brothers' toes were poking through their shoes. The twenty-five dollars we got for each of the dog's six puppies went toward the electricity bill, and when the tomatoes and beans and zucchini ripened in the yard, we saved even more. Whenever an unexpected check from my grandmother arrived in the mail, God was the one we thanked. But it also seemed like God must have preferred to keep us dependent on him, because even with all those prayers there was still never quite enough.

❧

Every Saturday my father packed us into the rusty yellow Datsun hatchback and we went house hunting, chasing classified ads for cheap rentals on the southern side of the county. The houses my father liked the best had lost their luster years ago. They'd been white once, but now the paint peeled off in patches and the flowerbeds were overrun with brambles. The insides of the houses were usually worse. The windows were drafty and the woodstove cantankerous, and sometimes the pantries and cabinets were still stuffed with someone else's trash. But my father grew more and more cheerful the more decrepit a house appeared. He preferred mildew to sterility—he didn't care if a house was rotten, he just wanted to know it was once alive. He loved those shabby houses the way he loved the broken-down cars everyone else passed over and only he could bring back to life, the way he loved the two-dollar rosebushes he bought on clearance at Snell's Feed and Farm. Others saw a clump of brown sticks, but he saw the green core underneath. In the same way, he overlooked the stains on the ceilings of those houses, their creaky foundations, the crumbling drywall, and the mouse droppings littering the sideboards. Instead he took in the carved banisters and brick hearths and wide parlors, the asparagus stalks that threaded through the weeds in the garden plot, the wide yard with space for rabbit pens and chicken coops and compost bins and whatever cars weren't running at the time.

One Saturday we finally found it. A ramshackle farmhouse with good bones, in the small hamlet of Olivet on the Patuxent River. And the price was right. When we pulled into the driveway my mother was already thanking the Lord. The couple who walked us through that house were old country people, land-poor with bad teeth, hands gnarled from arthritis, and threadbare clothes that hung off their thin frames. They raised their family in those rooms and planted the daffodils that sprang out of the ground every April and the apple trees that lined the eastern side of the house. But now the time had come to move in with their daughter's family, where they'd have a tidy little apartment with their own entrance and wouldn't have to unclog gutters any more or shovel snow.

The man gave us a slow, apologetic tour as his wife trailed behind, and you could hear the doubt in his voice as he told us about the problem with the plumbing in the downstairs bath and the loose floorboards on the front porch. My father played his part, knotting up his brow at the termite damage on the second floor and wincing at the live wiring, scuffing his feet and talking in low, troubled tones to my mother, all the while winking at my brothers and me. When the tour finally ended, the man hung his head and coughed nervously into his elbow, said maybe their oldest daughter was right. People nowadays wanted two bathrooms and a rec room. The house wouldn't rent, maybe best just to tear it down.

That was when my father ran his calloused fingers over the edge of the crown molding and got down on his knees to inspect the pipes under the sink. He told Obere to run to the car for his toolbox, and then he crawled into the midst of all those mouse droppings and fiddled around with the pipe until he found the loose bolt he was looking for and rejiggered the fittings so the sink would drain.

My father wiped the dust off his jeans and began talking brightly of other possible repairs, how he'd done a similar chimney job not long ago, how the porch could easily be reinforced. It became clear to the homeowners that this man had a genius for woodstoves and plumbing and wiring, that with his own grit and a monthly rent deduction, he could rebuild chimneys and build decks and rewire the back bedrooms.

When my father finally shook hands with the white-haired couple, my brothers and I high-fived each other behind my mother's back. We had already inventoried the musty outbuildings and discovered the frayed rope that marked the best branch for a swing on the locust tree. We'd tested the warped planks that bridged the creek in the backyard and decided they could be trusted with our weight, at least for a while longer. We found the spot on the main porch where my father could land every evening after he silenced the engine on the Ford and hauled himself out of the truck, where he could sip a Ball jar of my mother's iced tea and listen to the sound of the mourning doves as they perched on the power lines and inhale that sweet-smelling air as it came in from the river. I could see him there already, taking off his sweaty shirt and putting his feet up on a log or stool, watching my brothers roar up and down the dirt driveway in their Big Wheels, listening to my mother sing old hymns through the screen door as she did the dishes. When his mind was finally clear of the day, he would stretch and circle the yard, touching the leaves of the younger fruit trees and making sure the deer were staying clear of the vegetable garden.

When moving day finally came we packed our things in the cast-off banana boxes my mother had gotten from the grocery store. There were hundreds of books: my mother's canning manuals and self-help digests and homeschooling textbooks, my father's Louis L'Amour novels and car-repair guidebooks and whole shelves of Bibles—my father's navy blue Revised Standard edition engraved with his legal name, the one that no one ever called him. My mother's olive-green Living Bible, the one she pored over every morning before she put her makeup on. My brothers' Bibles, with graphic pictures of bloody battle scenes, the pocket Gideon Bibles with bright leather bindings in primary colors, and my own white Precious Moments edition.

There was the canopy bed I slept in, the one my father bartered from a client for a flagstone walkway, the china cabinet from my grandmother packed with mismatched glasses and plates from tag sales, the delicate coffee table with its spindly legs that my brothers regularly turned over in their wrestling matches. My brothers' BB guns and bows and arrows, racks of mason jars for canning tomatoes, the record player and the black-and-white TV we used for videos after my father snapped the antenna in protest of some raunchy sitcom. And all the animals we'd accumulated—parakeets and fish and guinea pigs, my beloved tan-colored cat and all his less-loved feline companions, an old basset hound named Bessie, and Sam's Jack Russell terrier.

The day of the move my mother and I went to work on the new house, scouring on our hands and knees, and back at Nostalgia my father and my uncle loaded up his truck high with furniture, boxes, and garbage bags of clothes, filling the cab with vases and houseplants. When the truck pulled up, Obere and Sam and I made an assembly line into the living room while my mother hurried around the house with rags and a bucket of Lysol, making final preparations. Once we had all those boxes piled up in the living room, my brothers scrambled over the heap looking for the boxes that held light bulbs and towels. The first piece of furniture my father put up was the long blond wood table he made from cast-off scraps, stained now from finger paints and burn scars from hot pans.

It seemed like we had just started unpacking when my mother called us to the table and stood over us at the sink to make sure we got every bit of grime out from under our fingernails. At the table we perched on mismatched stools and chairs and held hands for grace. My father always started his prayers with silence, and in that silence we struggled to keep our eyes squeezed closed, breathless from the scramble to the sink. Finally, my father cleared his throat and talked to the Lord like a friend. He thanked God for helping us find this house, for the good weather, and for keeping us safe through the move. He blessed each one of us by name, and then blessed the food and instructed it to nourish our bodies. Then he said, "Thank you, Father," and we knew enough to stay silent until he finally said, "Amen."

In that long minute of quiet the deeper silence finally settled inside of us. We saw the orange glow of the lamplight through our half-closed eyes, the silhouettes of my father and mother with their heads bent over paper plates. The most important things were all unpacked—toothbrushes and pajamas and silverware. At that moment it seemed like there would always be another farmhouse out there, when-ever we needed one, and we'd always be together. We were a healthy distance from anyone who meant us harm, so we imagined that no harm would come to us. It seemed like the world rested in the web of streets between the church and the grocery store, and back then that was enough. We didn't yet know there was a whole other world out there, gleaming and glittering, hungry to take us in.

※ *Chapter 3* ※

Upon This Rock

We loved that house, but we couldn't keep it. We went from house to house in those years, thirteen in all, moving whenever the landlord raised the rent or sold out to developers. It didn't matter though, because throughout all of it there was only one church. Rock Church of Southern Maryland sat in the middle of the county, in a run-down brick building in Broomes Island that used to be the Black elementary school back in the days before the schools were integrated. The church was led by a pastor who believed God could speak to him direct as any man. His name was Jim Cucuzza. He'd never been to divinity school and had no special letters before or after his name. His teeth were yellow and crooked and the three suits he rotated through were polyester, off the rack. In another life he worked construction, but now he was saved. The Bible was his guide and that was the only credential my parents needed. We followed him the way sheep follow a shepherd when the air cools and night is coming.

My parents didn't look like Holy Rollers. My mother wore jeans and permed her hair, dabbed perfume behind her ears on Sundays, unlike the doe-eyed Pentecostal women we sometimes saw at gas stations, who had long straight hair and ankle-length skirts. My father's thick black hair was longer than you might expect, and he was known to sip a beer on a hot day and take some chew if the guys at the construction site were offering. But five years before my birth, my mother and my father joined hands in a backyard in Virginia while a bearded preacher walked them through the salvation prayer. The preacher grasped my father's rough hands and told him that if he meant that prayer with all his heart, then when he rose from his knees he would become part of the kingdom, marked with God's own invisible mark.

Before that moment my parents felt alone and adrift in the world. My mother's father had been an alcoholic who died when she was sixteen years old after a lengthy separation from his family, and my father's father had died of a heart attack when he was only six years old. But when they repeated those words and rose up to standing they were changed. The world that had seemed so harsh and irrational was actually stitched together with love and care by a benevolent Lord who claimed them as a son and daughter. When they learned that it wasn't biblical to live together before marriage, my father packed his things up and found another place to sleep until they got married a year later. Once they joined the church they were part of a community. On Sundays there was a warm room full of songs and laughter, hearty handshakes and hugs with pats on the back, women who passed baby clothes and canned goods around to each other, men who teamed up to fix each other's trucks. And now there was this church—the same spirit in a different congregation.

There were dozens of other places to worship in the county, Methodist and Catholic, Baptist and Free Baptist, Bible-believing like us and against abortion and evolution and the homosexual agenda, but Pastor Jim liked to say those churches were dead. Day after day they just ran through the same routine, singing numbered hymns out of a dusty old book, reciting the same repeat-after-me prayer and listening to the same old sermons, and then those people walked out of that church no different than they were when they first walked in.

"You won't believe this," Pastor Jim told us one Sunday morning, pacing the edge of the altar in that converted gymnasium, tossing his tie over his shoulder, "but when those Christians get sick or lose their jobs or their marriages fall apart, they view it as a natural thing! Just a part of life!"

From her perch in the first row of folding chairs, Jeannette Camps waved a tambourine in his direction. I listened wide-eyed from a back row, taking notes in my unpracticed cursive handwriting so I could study his words later. Even then I knew better than those lukewarm, so-called Christians. Nothing happened without a reason. If you were beset by trials and tribulations, then you were a victim of spiritual warfare. Maybe the Devil himself edged up to God and said, This Christian of yours is only faithful because things are going pretty well. I say we test her. And the ever-patient Lord shrugged and said, Okay, test her then. But she'll stick by me. And the Devil sniggered and threw everything he had at that poor Christian. Disease and poverty, persecution. But if the Christian kept praising God and thanking him, even for the trials, then the Lord would reward her. Maybe on earth, and maybe in heaven.

"That's a promise," Pastor Jim said. "A promise you can cash in. Your reward might come here in this life or it might come later, but I'll tell you now, there are blessings in store for you, beyond anything you've ever known."

The men who sat in those folding chairs listening to the pastor were men like my father. They wore beards and often came to church with concrete-flecked hands and mud-caked boots. The women were like my mother, tender and shy, with out-of-fashion haircuts and thrift-store styles. They believed a woman's place was in the home, obeying her husband and guiding her children toward the truth. They struggled daily to put food on the table and when they felt scared or alone it was God they cried out to, not some charity. Definitely not the government. Like my parents, they clapped their hands over their children's ears when the six o'clock news came on, with its stories of the crack epidemic that raged in Washington, DC, and some New Yorker who dared to submerge a photograph of a crucifix in urine and call it art. If these people felt left out of a world that was changing faster than they could blink, with its shifting economy and super-computers and the first whispers about the World Wide Web, they could remind themselves that this world was always falling short of its creator. That was why they chose this church, because Pastor Jim preached that in a world that seemed empty and cold and unfeeling, promises had been made, promises that would be kept. Those who mourned on earth would be comforted later, in heaven. Eventually the meek would inherit the earth. People like us, who were persecuted and judged because of our faith, would gain admittance to the kingdom, and those out in the world, who soaked up its sinful culture and accepted the Devil's false promises, would be doomed to hellfire.

Pastor Jim and his wife and three daughters had been sent
to southern Maryland by Bishop John Gimenez, the head of
Rock Christian Fellowship. The bishop grew up in Span-
ish Harlem and overcame drug addiction and sin, following
the unspoken Pentecostal maxim that a man of God could
only rise as high in the spiritual kingdom as the depths that
he had fallen to before he took God into his heart. Before
he came to the county, Pastor Jim was Bishop Gimenez's
right-hand man. Almost ten years before, in 1980, they had
worked with Pat Robertson to put on Washington for Jesus,
a rally in which three hundred thousand Christians united
on the National Mall to pray that God would have mercy on
our sinful nation. Pastor Jim was the communications man
for the event, laying power lines and coordinating with the
media. After the rally was over he and the other deputies
were given orders to go forth from the bishop's church in
Virginia Beach, south and east and in every other direction.
Pastor Jim and his family went out on prayer to seed the
Rock Church of Southern Maryland, which meant they had
thrown themselves on the mercy of God and had no guarantee of a salary or a roof over their heads. I think that's
what my father liked most about Pastor Jim. He wasn't
building a church where you reported to a board of directors
or followed manmade regulations about how to behave. Instead he listened for the voice of the Lord to come barreling
through, and he followed it wherever it led.

Sunday after Sunday in that dingy gymnasium-turned-
sanctuary, I squirmed beside my parents watching big-eyed
as our pastor paced the edge of the threadbare stage. He
preached about a time when the Lord cleaved close to men
and walked among them, speaking to them in their own
language, often rattling them up a bit before they could hear

him. A burning bush. A staff softening into a snake. A fleece wet by morning on the dry ground. A dead man walking. But then the centuries rolled by and the voice of the Lord seemed to fade.

Pastor Jim stopped at the edge of the altar, gripping his microphone and cocking his head at one of the elders. "Was God just tired of talking?" he asked. "Had the Lord said enough?

"No, brothers and sisters," he answered in a quiet voice, pulling his eyeglasses off and blotting his forehead with a stained handkerchief. "The Lord had plenty to say. But we stopped listening and fell to sin instead. We had eyes but we did not see; we had ears but we did not hear."

Our pastor paged through his Bible and called out scriptures, arguing that we were in the season of Pentecost, close to the great and terrible end. He read from the Book of Revelation of the hidden manna and the white garments and the new names, the lake of fire and the solitary eagle, the locusts and the bottomless pit. He said that just before the coming trials and tribulations, before the sun turned to darkness and the moon to blood, the righteous would be carried up into the air. And then he reminded us that no one knew the day or hour of the Lord's return. We could only know the end was coming from the signs we were given. Nation would rise up against nation and there would be war and rumors of war. Pastor Jim counseled us to follow the example of the five wise virgins from the book of Matthew, who keep their lamps full of oil because the bridegroom might return at any moment. If our lamps flickered out and we forgot the Lord's commandments, we'd be barred from the wedding feast. We were sure we didn't have long to wait. All the signs were there—plagues were spreading in the northern cities, earthquakes rattled Central America and Asia, the United Nations was gaining power, and rumor had it a red heifer had been born in Jerusalem. The Lord was already equipping his faithful for the last days. Young men were seeing visions, old men were dreaming dreams, and God himself was blessing his people with the gift of strange tongues.

ɤ

One Sunday, Pastor Jim told us a story about a dream he had just before the Washington for Jesus rally. In the dream, he followed three men up a hill on a snowy day, and they were all dressed in the same clothing the soldiers wore during the Revolutionary War. The one in the front held an American flag, and at one point he turned to Pastor Jim and said, "This is your Valley Forge."

Pastor Jim spread his arms wide to encompass the whole sanctuary. He said that right now we were in our own Valley Forge. We were in the midst of a long winter. We suffered, and some went hungry. Some doubted. But it would all be worth it. We would triumph at last. We would fight as one people against the spirit of greed, which blossomed in the middle of our government like a cancerous tumor, and the spirit of poverty, which kept us poor and ashamed. We would trust the Lord and crush the spirits of fear under our feet. We would build a new church on a hill, where everyone could see it, a church that would stand fast against the gates of hell.

We sat at the edge of our seats and looked around. We saw, as if for the first time, the yellowed walls, the cracks in the linoleum, the stains on the brown carpet in the tiny fellowship hall, the rusty folding chairs we sat in twice on Sundays and once on Wednesday nights. We opened our minds and for the first time tried to imagine a building truly worthy of our Lord. A church bigger than the county courthouse or the Catholic parish up the street, sitting tall and proud on a hill. It would have a baptismal font, a playground, and a fresh carpet that wasn't stained from school children's accidents or Sunday afternoon potlucks.

It turned out Pastor Jim already had a site in mind, a plot of land on a hill in Saint Leonard, at the intersection of Ball Road and Route 4. Even before the title was signed, one of the elders took the enormous rock that sat outside our old church in Broomes Island and borrowed a bulldozer to lift it up and transport it to its new home on the hill. On Easter morning we held a sunrise service out there beside it, trussed up in flannels and wools, the wind whipping our faces, Pastor Jim shouting the sermon from the top of a hay bale. He told us the story of how Jesus's friends came to find him after his crucifixion, to anoint his dead body with oils and fragrant herbs. But then they found that the gravestone had been rolled away.

Pastor Jim stepped down off the hay bale and walked around to each one of us. He said in a soft voice, "That stone was rolled away for you. And you, and you, and you. That stone was rolled away so you could live a life of freedom. So you would be saved from eternal hellfire. It was out of mercy that Christ died for you."

We stood there on that Easter morning with the sun rising at our backs and the wind whistling onto our red cheeks and consecrated that land. Christ died for us and the least we could do was build him a church that would bring the whole county to Jesus. It was Pastor Jim who first gave us the seed of the idea, but we watered it and weeded it and prepared the soil. Over the next three years we gave every dollar we had, then gave our Saturdays to dig and pave and trim and work that land into something that could serve as a solid foundation. In that congregation were plumbers and roofers and tile men and bricklayers like my father, and every Saturday they laced their still-damp work boots up and headed to the land. The wives formed committees to serve up sandwiches and paint walls, and even my brothers and I pitched in, digging the parking lot and cleaning up trash. And when all of it was done we gave a dozen more Saturdays and built Pastor Jim and his family a house on that same plot of land.

❦

When the church was finally done, it was the newest thing my brothers and I had ever seen. The night we dedicated it, Bishop John Gimenez himself drove up from Virginia Beach with his wife, Anne, a slim brunette with a Texas twang and a singing voice like someone from the radio. He was a thick man with a ready smile, and he and Sister Anne sat in plush, high-backed chairs during the worship service. When it was time for the sermon, Pastor Jim told stories of the bishop's exploits by way of an introduction—the church he built in Virginia Beach with only the hand of the Lord helping him, the way he and Pat Robertson packed the National Mall with hundreds of thousands of Christians, the churches he'd planted in far-off Africa and Asia and everywhere in between.

But when the bishop rose to speak, he walked past Pastor Jim and stood silent in the middle of that long, pink-carpeted altar, quiet for nearly thirty seconds. Through his dark aviator-style glasses he gazed at the skylights, the deep mauve of the carpet of the sanctuary, the textured wallpaper, the overflow room off the sanctuary. He even turned around and sized up the baptismal font with its blue-tinged chlorinated water and the stones lining the wall behind it, rose-colored stones from a quarry in Virginia that my father cut to fit and laid by hand. For as long as we could bear the bishop just stood there. My father peered around and shrugged when he caught Elder Knoll's eye, but then the bishop dropped to his knees and raised his arms to that forty-foot tall ceiling, and shouted in his tremendous voice, "Hallelujah, Jesus!" The praise and worship team put a trill into the keyboard and hit the chimes and played a long, low trumpet note, and just like that everyone in that enormous sanctuary cried out and praised the Lord in the highest timbres their voices could reach. My brothers and I looked on wide-eyed as Betty Sams danced a jig and Elder Shenberger reached for his wife's hand and skipped down the aisle.

My father raised his hands to the sky and rocked back and forth on his toes. My mother prayed in her quiet way, her hands on my brother's shoulders as she sang sweetly in tongues under her breath. That whole place shook for hours that night, and Bishop Gimenez didn't get to preaching until nine o'clock or so. When he did he spit fire from his mouth as he blessed the church and poured oil over every bit of the altar. He told us of the seven evil spirits that afflicted America, that were here somewhere in this town, here in this room with us even—the persecution of Christians, homosexuality, abortion, racism, addiction, the occult, and HIV/AIDS. He said when you put those letters together they spelled PHARAOH, and that meant the Devil was triumphing in America today just as he had once before in ancient Egypt.

The way he talked it sounded like what Pastor Jim told us was true. There was a war going on, and we were on the front lines. The cars that pulsed across Route 4 downhill from the sanctuary held people who were just going about their business, buying groceries, visiting grandchildren, heading to the movies. Seeking sensation. In their deepest heart of hearts they burned to know the Lord, but they remained strangers to him. No Christian had ever told them about what God could do for them. And that made them vulnerable to the Enemy. Even as he spoke the Devil was laying a trap and luring them, by way of alcohol or greed or lust, and off they went into his waiting hands. God wanted to save them, but he needed us to be his helpers. It was up to us to speak out and tell them another way. To witness.

Bishop Gimenez asked us if we thought we could get over ourselves, move past fear and embarrassment and just use plain, simple words to tell them about another way, to tell them about the work God did in each and every one of us, the way he took the old and scraped it out and let it fall away, the way he made us clean again, white as snow. We told him we would.

By the time the night was over, the bishop had told so many stories of spirits crushed and conquered and had given so many prophecies that I couldn't quite figure out which spirits were already bound up and which battles were still ahead of us. Toward eleven o'clock, my brothers fell asleep, Obere on the floor, wrapped in my father's suit jacket, and Sam with his head in my mother's lap. I sat next to my father, listening and taking notes, scribbling furiously just like my mother with a ballpoint pen, recording all the promises and blessings. The bishop prayed over Pastor Jim, that he would be a good and mighty man, and then prayed over all the leadership, and then of course there was an altar call, with a few souls saved.

When the time came for rededicating our lives to the Lord we all poured down to the altar. The bishop came around to anoint each one of us, his thumbs dabbing our foreheads with oil, shaking and pressing the Lord into our temples and cursing the demons who could take our peace away. When he lifted his broad hands from my head I could still feel his thumbprints, and when I rubbed my forehead with my palm I could see the sheen of that holy oil. I squared my shoulders and followed my mother back to our seats.

It was midnight when the dedication service was over. Sam drooped over my father's broad shoulders and Obere tottered hand in hand with my mother, my father's suit jacket shrouding him like a lank-limbed child ghost. My father laid his heavy palm on the back of my neck as we walked toward the car. All around us engines rumbled to life, the exhaust smoke shimmering in the chilly November air. My father packed us into the hatchback and rolled his window down to clasp hands with one of the deacons before we left. When we turned onto Route 4, I craned my neck around to take one more look at that big church on the hill. Someone had set up spotlights on the letters that adorned the side of the church, letters bearing the inscription, "Upon this rock I will build my church, and the gates of hell shall not prevail against it." I watched the glow fade into the night as we made our way down the dark highway.

Chapter 4

Revival

A few years after the church was built, Pastor Jim said we were all getting lazy and bloated with sin, like the cattle in Pharaoh's dream. We needed to sanctify ourselves, to wash all that worldly doubt and dirt away and get right with God again. Only then could the Lord do a great work in us. So the deacons pitched a big white tent near a corn-field in Port Republic, borrowed a couple of generators, and bought straw bales from the Amish to serve as a floor. I must have been ten years old and all week the prospect of that big white tent loomed large in my mind. Over breakfast my mother asked me four times to pass the maple syrup and I just stared at her unblinking, thinking maybe tonight would be the night when I finally got the gift of tongues.

Pastor Jim had told us so many times that the ability to speak in tongues was pure grace, but I knew better. Baptism was kid stuff. Anyone who recited the words to the salvation prayer could make an appointment to receive the sacrament on the third Sunday of every month. But the gift of tongues was from the Holy Ghost himself. He knew your innermost thoughts, and only if you were pure would he make a home in your heart and bless you with supernatural gifts—the gift of prophecy or healing, the gift of tongues or the ability to interpret tongues. I wanted all those gifts for myself, to hoard them like spiritual badges of honor. It was frustrating to me that there was no timeline for sanctification. The gifts could come to anyone, anywhere, at any time. I knew a woman once who received her prayer language while leaning over to remove a cauliflower casserole from the oven. The Lord struck her with great force, and when her mouth opened God's words came out instead of her own.

When we gathered for worship as a congregation, anyone with ears to hear could tell who had the Holy Spirit and who didn't. Those who were blessed with a new language lifted their chins proudly and howled it to the heavens; while those who were stuck with English tucked their heads and mumbled boring words anyone could understand. My parents already had the gift. My father's prayer language was guttural and vaguely Germanic, and my mother's was higher-toned and melodic. But no matter how hard I prayed, God would not give me a latter-day language of my own.

※

By the time I finished my breakfast, the sun struck the top of the eastern windows in the dining room, bathing us in its buttery light and illuminating the dust motes in the air. Last night's dishes were still piled high in the sink, the litter box was dirty and the wood box empty, but it was still early in the day, and my mother was optimistic that all the tasks she had charted out for us in her cursive handwriting would still be completed, and she'd manage to finish the laundry and get dinner on the table and iron her dress for the revival.

She called out to us from the living room and we came running, squabbling about who got to sit next to her for our morning devotions, the start to our day of homeschooling. Obere and I won like we always did, and Sam perched on the side of the couch. I curled up beside my mother, squinting through my bottle-cap glasses, knobby knees tucked under me, one hand resting on my mother's pregnant belly in case the baby kicked. She placed one hand on my neck while she read from her well-thumbed, olive-green Bible.

Today it was one of our favorites, the story of Daniel, a man of God who was sentenced to a night in the lions' den by a jealous king. But then an angel of the Lord closed up the lions' mouths so they couldn't touch him. My brothers gaped at each other and my mother kept reading, telling us how the king was so impressed by Daniel's witness that he decided to throw all his evil advisors into the den along with their children and wives, and the lions leaped upon them and tore them apart before they even hit the bottom of the den. And then the king ordered everyone to tremble in fear in front of God. Obere asked my mother to read it again, but I squirmed. It didn't sound like that was something God should do—throw children to lions. But then there was a blur of hands and elbows and Sam fell off the couch with a thud and my mother shouted at Obere. She told us to close our eyes and we suspected that after the final prayer she'd cancel school for the day if we promise to double up on math and reading on Monday.

When we were free, the boys raced out of the house and set off for the creek. I ambled through the garden to see if anything was ripe and then climbed onto the rope swing my father had built. I started turning the story of Daniel around in my head as I kicked off the locust tree. If God could save Daniel from the lions, then why didn't he save Obere from the German shepherd who took a piece out of his leg when he was biking in front of the house last week? Maybe Obere wasn't pure enough. Maybe God wanted to teach him a lesson. I thought about the children in the lions' den, the ones who got torn apart. I wondered if they died in the fall. I hoped so. And then I wondered if that was the right thing to hope. Maybe God didn't want anyone feeling sorry for them.

The rope on the swing got tangled up and I spun around in tight circles trying to get it free. Maybe I hadn't gotten the gift yet because the Holy Spirit had read me like a book and saw everything that was wrong with me. I wished I was an only child. I thought I was the smartest person around. I read the books about the evils of pornography that my mom ordered from the American Family Association, and when I lay in bed at night I turned those images over in my head.

I heard voices coming over the hill down by the chicken coop and Obere ran toward me, Sam following closely behind.

"I want a turn!" Obere said.

I was instantly furious. "Leave me alone! Go away!"

His face fell and he shrank away, grabbing Sam by the shoulder and pulling him along with him. My eyes burned. I tried so hard to be good and I just couldn't manage to do it.

The screen door slammed and my mother stepped outside with the wicker hamper on her hip, piled high with wet towels. She called out to me and I slumped over to her, pushing my hair out of my face.

"Grab those clothespins, honey," she said. I reached for them and handed them over but stayed silent. She was humming some stray tune under her breath and her face had that washed-clean look that she got whenever she'd had a half hour to herself to read the Bible and pray.

"What's wrong?"

I shrugged. She searched my face and then put the hamper down and took my hand. She deposited me on a wicker chair on the porch and disappeared into the kitchen, returning with a glass of iced tea.

"I don't understand," I said. "Why would God let the kids be eaten by the lions?"

I remember the way she smelled then, like oranges and pine-scented dish soap, and I remember that she held me close, but whatever words she used are lost to memory. It was probably something about how God's ways are his ways and sometimes our minds are too small to understand the great plans he has for our lives. But the words didn't matter. The fact of her presence was enough to soothe me.

ⓦ

When we heard our father's truck pull in that evening, we raced into the yard, the screen door banging behind us and the terrier barking furiously about being left inside. But my father didn't look at us, and he just grunted when we asked if he had brought anything home. He snapped at my mother when she tried to hurry him into the shower to get dressed for church. Sam and I looked at her questioningly and she shrugged and told us to go upstairs and get ready. When we came back downstairs, the smell of burnt hamburger wafted in from the kitchen and Obere was loading the wood box with a tear-stained face.

We weren't sure what had happened. Anything could have set my father off—his life was balanced on such a precarious point that so many different things could have gone wrong. A fight with one of his clients, probably, or traffic on the Beltway. Maybe a potential client had turned down a quote because he didn't carry insurance. Or sometimes his moods had nothing to do with any of that at all. Maybe he was just wrestling with his own demons on the long ride home from Virginia, and maybe something about our faces had reminded him of something in his past that he would have liked to have forgotten.

Sometimes it felt like our whole lives rocked on the axis of his moods. It didn't take very much to get our father thundering like some Old Testament prophet. Whenever we saw his storms forming, my brothers and I sought small spaces, tucking ourselves into the fold of the long closet under the attic stairs, breathing in that mothball smell, and running our fingers along the mottled plaster. Or we'd slip out the front door and make for the weedy strip of gravel under the tall boxwoods that lined the front of the house. If his thundering reached a particular level, we'd run for the empty silo in the barn next door and curl up at the bottom, watching the swallows cut into the blue circle of sky above us. But sometimes he'd spy an ankle as we ran by him, glimpse a curl of my hair from under the boxwoods, and then he'd rush after us, all the while yelling. We were bad, we would always do the wrong thing if presented with a choice, there was no way to right us, not even the rod would right us, though he would certainly try to right us, and we would sink lower and lower with every shout, as if his voice was a post-hole digger driving us down into the ground.

\~

An hour later, when the five of us finally piled into the Datsun hatchback, Obere's eyes were still a little red. He'd refused to wear socks until my father threatened to take off the belt he had just put on. My mother wore a freshly ironed dress with blue and red roses on it, a little gel in her hair, and a splash of drugstore perfume. My father had managed to scrape the dried-up concrete out of the hair on the back of his hands and traded his work boots for the dress shoes I'd shined the day before. He steered the car with one finger and eyed Obere in his perch in the middle of the bench seat in the back. My mother talked brightly to lighten the mood.

Slowly we made our way down a ten-mile stretch of highway, the pitch-black woods hugging us on either side. The Chesapeake Bay flowed just beyond those woods to the west and the Patuxent River wound around to the east, and the revival was in a borrowed patch of field that was cut out of the woods. My father nosed the hatchback into a parking spot and we all piled out and filed into that glowing tent. We took our places in a row of chairs toward the back, set the Bibles down, and joined in the singing.

Back at church we sang worship songs that sounded like pop music, but tonight in the tent Miss Kathy led the band through the old hymns, the ones everyone knew by heart—"Amazing Grace," "What a Friend We Have in Jesus," "There Is a Balm in Gilead." My father took my mother's arm. She resisted at first, then he caught her eyes and they smiled secret, closed-lip smiles. My mother's lilting soprano joined my father's baritone and even Obere fell in line with the melody. My heart lifted in my chest and for the first time all day I felt like I could breathe. I closed my eyes with relief and lifted my voice with the music, clapping until the palms of my hands stung. Then we stretched our hands toward the top of that white tent, and those who had the gift spoke in that beautiful heavenly language that came from the Holy Spirit. For a minute, it felt like the Lord himself might come down to meet us.

There was so much we wanted in that moment. We wanted to tap into the force that spun mountains and oceans out of air and take it into us. We wanted to know all the names for God. We wanted to speak in a language we couldn't understand. We wanted to burn away our old selves and peel off the burned skin and find new skin there. We wanted to grow like seeds in the light of God's all-encompassing presence. We wanted to make heaven here on the earth. We wanted to confront evil and blot it out. We wanted to be bigger than any single one of us could be on our own. We wanted to be pure.

Outside that glowing tent it was the mid-eighties and the world marched in sync to the plans already laid out in the Book of Revelation. Madonna strutted around in a studded leather bra and Michael Jackson moonwalked, but none of our families had cable and we wouldn't know those songs until later. There were two types of people out there, believers and doubters, and to the believers God promised every good thing. But still we had to be vigilant. Too often the daily interfered, and we ended up doing and saying things we didn't mean, things that didn't line up with who we wanted to be. Sin was always tempting and luring us away, and with that came a susceptibility to sickness and disease. I had the feeling that if I left the halo of light and moved closer to the woods, any kind of evil could creep up and slip under my skin. It was true that I was redeemed by the blood of the lamb. I read my Bible and prayed every day, but that didn't mean I was entirely safe. I needed to stay close to the fire so I'd stay pure. Outside the circle of light you just never know.

The guest minister had come up from North Carolina or Tennessee. He combed his eyes over us and spoke quietly and seriously about the evil that lurked somewhere among us. There were some out there in the crowd, he said, who were possessed by the spirit of hypocrisy—they acted like Christians on Sunday and didn't think of God a bit until the end of the week.

"There's someone here tonight," he said, his voice growing louder, "someone who believes they can hide their sins from God and their community, and I tell you now they're wrong!" A thin man I didn't know very well slipped past his wife and daughters and made his way to the altar, and then started shaking and crying. Suddenly a quiet descended, and the congregation's separate attentions funneled together. And still the guest minister kept going, calling out all kinds of spirits, all kinds of struggles. Somewhere among us was a child with a rash on his cheeks, a woman with female troubles, a man whose back was keeping him up at night. He shouted the words, his voice hoarse with emotion. Sweat poured off his face and his hair was matted and wet. But healing was possible! You just had to get down on your knees and repent.

He called out all the sins in the world, like he was taking attendance, and when people's numbers came up they headed for the altar. I fixed my eyes on the floor. I was shy, but when the minister named the sin of pride something caught in my throat. I thought about how I felt when I overheard my dad bragging about me to his clients or our neighbors, telling them how I'd learned to read when I was four and then skipped second grade.

"Put it on the altar," the guest minister said gently, and it was like he was talking to me. "Let him take it. You'll be okay without it."

My heart raced faster. I swallowed hard and got up to brush past my family, but there was no one left in the row but me. I spotted my mother on one side of the altar, her hands on her belly, head bowed. She prayed out loud and clasped her hands. My father was a few steps away from her, his hands lifted. He tilted back and forth on his heels as he prayed and his eyes were closed.

The minister kept at it until all the folding chairs were empty. He made his way down the row with Pastor Jim and some of the elders, and before long we felt calloused hands gripping our temples, blessing us and pardoning us, driving out any lurking spirits. People keeled over and fell out, rent motionless by the sheer emotional force of it all. They were like balloons that had suddenly deflated. Their leg muscles went weak and their core collapsed, and their eyes fluttered and closed. They were there one minute and the next minute they were with God.

I watched Obere fall under the weight of the pastor's hand. One moment my brother was standing there beside me and the next moment he'd darted backward in his cowboy boots, hitting the ground with all the force of a man, his head knocking back into the dust. I wondered what sins he whispered about to God. Leaving my father's tools out in the rain? Pushing Sam off the couch?

I wanted to fall too, more than anything. But when my turn came and the pastor pushed at my forehead and the deacons stood behind me at the ready, my legs refused to give out. I squeezed my eyes shut and tried to put my thoughts to sleep. I knew that if I could just let go, then I could get the blessing too. But my mind darted around and I couldn't get a handle on it. I was already thinking of the next thing—what my knees would do when I fell, whether my skirt would come up and show my underpants. And then the thought flashed through my head—maybe I couldn't fall because my belief wasn't pure; it was salt and pepper mixed together. I had all these nagging questions and doubts, and that must have been why the Spirit passed me by.

My face went red and my eyes filled up with tears. The pastor grimaced and moved on to the elderly man next to me, and I stood there by myself in my saddle shoes, wishing I too could have been swept away by the Spirit. Beside me the deacons shook choir robes over the women's legs as they lay there dumb in the straw.

Chapter 5

The Beach

Early one Saturday morning when I was twelve, my father rustled me awake. I patted my bedside table for my tortoise-shell glasses, then rose heavy-footed to pull on a sweatshirt and lace up my sneakers. Out in the hallway the new baby cried out sharply from my mother's room, and the bed creaked as she turned over to find him in the blankets and put him to her chest. I maneuvered past the sleeping dogs on the floor of the kitchen and tiptoed over the detritus of muddy boots and Legos. A dead white patch of fluorescent light over the kitchen sink illuminated a mass of dishes, and the smell of last night's grease turned my stomach.

But when I made my way into the yard and took in the cold, clean night air, the sleep drained out of my head immediately. I climbed into the truck and the high rumble of the muffler echoed through the morning mist. When my father made the right onto Route 4, his fingers found the radio knob. The early morning talk show hosts gave their commentary about all the things people had said and done to each other the week before, and we wound our way through those dark roads, passing Southern Calvert Baptist and the

AME church and dozens of tobacco farms, the plants barely visible beneath the mist. At the 7-Eleven on the corner of Routes 231 and 4, bearded men in camouflage jackets sipped from Styrofoam cups of coffee as they gassed up, raising a two-fingered salute at the passing cars.

We pulled off the highway on Sixes Road and wound through the farms, pulling into the driveway of a white farmhouse more expansive than ours. A pair of twin girls slumped against each other on the porch swing. Like me, they were twelve years old, knobby-kneed, buck-toothed, and frizzy-haired, but Molly's hair was permed and Emmy had green-blue eyes so big and blank they seemed to take in the whole world. They crowded in next to me on the bench seat and my knees straddled the gear shift, Molly's bony hips pinning me from the right. None of us said a word as we followed the yellow lines of the road back to the main highway and another couple of miles south through Saint Leonard, then west toward the Chesapeake Bay until we finally reached that rough oyster-shell packed road at Calvert Beach. The tires crunched against the shells as my father parked on the side of the boat ramp and we girls piled out of the car, wrapping our sweatshirts tight around our scrawny arms.

The sun's early rays were already creeping out of the dark behind us, washing Molly's face of her freckles, turning our faces dark-blue in the dim light. The horizon reddened as morning grew into day, and only then did we shake off our silence and start darting around and chattering. The beach filled up with dog walkers and sharks'-teeth hunters, and we walked for a half-mile in the water-logged sand with the clay cliffs at our backs, trudging behind my father in our matching Converse sneakers, the horseflies buzzing around us and the sand fleas leaping onto our legs. When the sun finally brightened enough to warm our faces and light up the shapes of the shells and flotsam on the shore, my father taught us how to train our eyes for tiny dark triangles in the sand, until our pockets jingled with fossilized sharks' teeth. He showed us how to spot bald eagles in the tall trees that lined the cliffs beside the beach, and picked up a dead crab in the sand to teach us how you could tell a female by the painted fingernails at the tips of her claws.

Molly and Emmy only half-listened. They were more interested in scraping their names into the sand and scaring each other by picking up half-dead horseshoe crabs by their spiked tails and tossing them into the brackish water. Strangely my father didn't seem to mind. Out here on the beach he was long-suffering. If Molly wanted to try her hand with his old Mamiya camera and use half a roll of film to take pictures of her toes, he didn't snatch the camera away. Instead he took his time showing her how to adjust the aperture and set the shutter speed. When Emmy interrupted his monologue to ask if it was time to go get breakfast, he didn't give her the silent treatment, he just suggested we walk a little farther first.

While the twins looked for sticks to pierce the half-dead jellyfish, I paced closely behind my father. He was in his prime then—tall, black-bearded, broad-shouldered, his thick body mostly muscle. He knew the names of all the trees, sassafras and birch, poplar and oak. He could pick out a hawk from a quarter mile away or see the faintest splash in the milky-brown water and know if it was a skate or a rockfish or just a bit of flotsam. He did the same thing with people too, sizing them up in a minute, calling them weak, like most of his clients, or strong, like Pastor Jim. Years later I'd decide that was part of the reason why he chose the faith he did—it had a name and label for everything in the world. Certain things were clearly correct and right: honoring your elders, obeying your parents, submitting to your husband. And then there was pure evil: homosexuality, abortion, divorce. There was little room for neutrality, and that was a great comfort to my father. He had grown up without religion, without any kind of moral compass. His mother was a hard-living, chain-smoking waitress who had married five times. My father broke away from his family early on, and while he craved moral absolutes, he also had the notion that to succeed in the world, you needed to be savvy, not soft.

Maybe that was why, of all the ponytailed girls we ran around with at church, my father chose Molly and Emmy to bring along to the beach on Saturdays. Their father was out of the picture, and he saw some spunk in them, the same kind of spunk that had allowed him to overcome the loss of a father and make his way through the world alone. In my father's eyes, all the twins lacked was some technical knowledge of the world, awareness of what was what. Maybe he thought if he took them under his wing he could set them on the right track.

But even then it was too late. Molly and Emmy were already showing up for youth group with gold hoops swaying from their ears and sullen expressions, jean shorts pegged so high up their thighs that Miss Kathy, the youth group leader, made an impromptu decision to read from Proverbs 31, the chapter about the industrious woman. She stood in front of us in her bright polyester dress and pantyhose and feathered hair and reminded us of our goal, to be completely free of sin and blemish. To keep our lamps burning, like the wise virgins who know that Jesus can come at any moment. To remain pure, because that made us holy, and in holiness there was power. It was clear that if we were stained we would be useless.

I sat wide-eyed during Miss Kathy's presentation, trying to memorize the list of acceptable dating behaviors (hanging out with boys in groups, courtship) and the things that weren't okay (any kind of petting or kissing before marriage). The little I knew about sex came from the thick letters my parents received every week, mass-mailed from Colorado Springs and bearing the signature of Dr. James Dobson, the head of Focus on the Family. Every week the letters related another travesty—teenage pregnancy, child molesters, gay teachers trying to convert our youth. From those letters I knew that when two married people had sex, it was fine because the Lord wanted there to be more children in the world. But when sex went wrong—outside of marriage, in unnatural configurations, there was nothing the Lord hated more. I did my best to toe the line. The rare times that I dared to imagine the carnal act, I made sure to imagine a wedding first, so that it wasn't too sinful. When I pulled on my pajamas and found my mind drifting over to a wiry, brown-eyed boy in my youth group, I counted sheep to put those thoughts out of my mind. When he tracked me down in the parking lot one Sunday after church and asked me to be his girlfriend, I shook my head no and didn't dare to look up as he slunk away. I felt a dull thumping in my chest and knew this was sin, making itself alive and known to me. The entire next day, I stayed in bed with a feverish feeling. Whenever I thought of his hand in mine, guilt bubbled up from the pit of my belly.

🌿

By the time we started seventh grade, Molly and Emmy had lost interest in the beach. By then I'd finally convinced my parents to let me go to public school, and sometimes I'd run into them there. The assistant principal was always collaring them in the hallway, pulling out a ruler to make sure their shorts were only two inches above their knees. In gym class they knotted their T-shirts up so far that glimpses of neon sports bras flashed fluorescent against their flat, tan bellies. After school the twins sat outside on the brick wall by the line of buses, blending in with all the popular kids, until I gradually realized that they had become the popular kids and started hurrying past them. When their loud, lipsticked friends made fun of my turtlenecks and high-water jeans, the twins shut them up with a look and beckoned me over to catch up. Their voices softened when they asked about my dad, but I couldn't quite get my breath out and spoke in shy mono-syllables. When I saw them in the middle of that buzzing hive of girls, I didn't know where they learned to talk so loud or use language like that, because their mother was a quiet woman and my father always said their step-father was soft.

Maybe I would have followed the twins down that path if I had a little of their beauty, if I were a little curvier or more confident. But I had glasses and braces, a flat chest and a great mane of hair that frizzed up whenever I tried to style it. I was so thin my doctor instructed my mother to deep fry all of my food—even the vegetables—and told me to eat a peanut butter sandwich after lunch and dinner. While Molly and Emmy flirted with boys and learned to use mascara, I whiled away long hours reading novels in a blue beanbag chair in my bedroom, the only place I was free of my brothers' endless whooping and wrestling or my moth-er's pleas to go outside. I didn't eat peanut butter sandwiches and my mother didn't deep fry my vegetables. Instead I grew paler and skinnier and quieter by the day.

One day in that beanbag chair I came across a quarter-page advertisement in the *Calvert Independent* for four-year scholarships to the private high school at the northern side of the county. I pulled out the box of stationery my aunt had given me for Christmas and wrote a note in careful cursive asking for more materials, and a week later a thick manila envelope showed up in the rusty mailbox at the end of the driveway. Inside was an application for the Calverton School and a bound viewbook with thick, cream-colored pages. On the cover was a girl about my age with green eyes and straight yellow hair tied up in a ponytail. She was wearing a blue crewneck sweater and a plaid skirt, and she was the most beautiful girl I had ever seen. Inside the book were full-color photos of perfectly groomed children in navy-blue plaids and striped ties looming over microscopes and algae pools, wielding tennis rackets, sitting rapt as bow-tied professors scrawled on old-fashioned chalkboards.

Over lasagna a few nights later I built my case. I didn't talk about the free college counseling or SAT classes, the rigorous curriculum or the long lists of colleges where Calverton graduates had been accepted. I knew my mother well enough to know those were the last things she wanted to hear. She had no doubt that I would go on to college, just as she had, but she didn't want me to go to some far-away school. The state university had been good enough for her and my father—though he never finished his degree. And it would keep me close to home. So instead I focused on the alternative. Calvert High School was a dull brick building, the high school that all the middle schools in the southern part of the county fed into. Whenever we went to the McDonald's close to campus my mother pulled us close, away from the boys with saggy pants, the girls with tight ponytails and their hair shaved in the back, their insolent stares and belligerent laughter. I reminded them there were only two choices—Calverton or Calvert High School. And everyone knew that Calvert High School was a den of iniquity. The cops were always making drug busts in the parking lot. If I went there I'd be lucky to make it out alive, much less go to college.

My mother gave my father an uneasy glance, but he didn't notice. He wasn't really opposed to the idea of Calverton. He'd always been proud of my grades, and he frequently told the story of how, when I was four, I rifled through the china cabinet and found a reading kit my mother had ordered from a catalog and stowed away. When I nagged my mother to go over the lessons with me, she promised we'd start the following year. But I didn't listen. Instead I snuck into the box and tore through the workbooks, scuffing the covers and helping myself to the prizes. My mother was appalled, skeptical that any good could come from this hungry quality of mine.

Sam screeched for my mother to give him seconds and she scooped some more lasagna onto his plate. She said she wasn't sure about Calverton. She'd heard it was a pretty liberal school. They celebrated Halloween and most of the kids didn't go to church. I gulped and prattled on about Calverton's mission, stressing the honor code and their commitment to family values. For weeks I became newly helpful, taking a terry-cloth towel in hand and sticking by my mother's side, extemporizing about the value of education and helping her wipe surfaces and dry silverware. When she finally gave me permission to send over my handwritten essays, the kitchen glimmered.

The sticky, muggy weather crept by slowly as I waited to hear back from Calverton. My father's garden grew into flower and he paid me and my brothers a penny each to pick potato bugs off the potatoes and Japanese beetles off his roses. Obere quickly got bored, but I spent hours in the garden with an old coffee can full of soapy water. While I turned over the leaves of the rosebushes looking for beetles I dreamt about the next thing.

◊

My father's truck broke down again just before the admissions test for Calverton and a guidance counselor offered to pick me up. When I saw Miss Weems pull into our rutted driveway in a sporty red coupe, I suddenly felt embarrassed by the knee-high grass, the old refrigerator on the porch and the broken-down tractor in the middle of the yard, and my tow-headed baby brother, Joshua, who was playing on the edge of the porch clad in only a diaper.

Miss Weems wore lip liner and small, tasteful gold earrings. She had a stylish bob that curled under at the ends. When she turned on the engine, strains of classical music came out of the stereo. She asked if I wanted a mint and shook her head when I apologized for tracking mud in on the floor.

"That's fine, dear," she said, nodding briskly and moving the little leather trash bag from the passenger-side floorboard into the backseat. "I'm just glad I found this place! I thought that dirt road would never end." She rolled down the window and cooed goodbye to my mother, who stood on the corner of the porch waving exuberantly. I shivered at the blast of cold, pine-scented air that flowed from the vent. I hadn't been in a car with a working air-conditioner since my aunt visited from California a few years before.

"Such a charming spot," Miss Weems said, but her mouth looked grim. She maneuvered her way past the broken-down

Datsun and the cage of ducks in the yard, keeping an eye on the old mangy brown mutt that stood guard at the end of the driveway.

"I have to tell you, my dear, how thrilled we were to read your essays. Of course nothing is final yet, but I can say that you're just the student we're hoping to find. Someone who can thrive if they are placed in the right soil." She winked at me, and I told her how grateful I was for the opportunity to go to Calverton. It was like I had a script in front of me and I was reading my lines.

The tests went well, and a few months later my mom and I were in Walmart buying white and blue polo shirts. When I tried on those clothes in the stuffy fitting room my heart soared. I thought I'd blend in with the rest of the students and slip into the fold. But of course I was wrong. I knew that from the first day, when the teachers called roll. Parren, Weems, Briscoe, Ewalt, McNatt. Their names were all over town: etched on the signposts in front of local businesses or the steel plates in the lobby of the hospital that listed all the donors. When my turn came I mumbled my name. A tall, blond girl lifted her head and glared at me from the front of the room, and I recognized the girl on the cover of the viewbook. She looked me up and down and whispered something to the boy sitting next to her, and he snickered.

I knew then that I wasn't fooling anyone. My polo shirts were $5.99 each, three for twelve dollars. The material was missing the pockets everyone else's polo shirts had, and the buttons were made from plain white plastic, not patterned in white and brown. And there was no little horse on the right breast pocket, just a stamped monogram with the initials *FG* for Faded Glory, the Walmart brand. Even my cheap Bic pens gave me away. But I didn't give up entirely. Over the next four years I purged my speech of Southern lilts and sloppy grammar, carefully training myself to say *Washington* instead of *Warshington*, *refrigerator* instead of *icebox*. On casual Fridays, when my classmates wore silky sundresses and freshly ironed khakis, I put together bizarre combinations of colorful thrift store clothes and earned a reputation as an iconoclast. When my father's latest pickup truck came motoring into the parking lot an hour late, filled to the brim with landscaping equipment, I registered the amusement and pity in the headmaster's eyes and quickly said my goodbyes. I counted coins so I could join my classmates for field trips and pre-prom dinners. I winced when the tears ran down Pastor Jim's face on Sunday mornings when he spoke of the blessings of the Lord, when my classmates at school asked why I wasn't allowed to celebrate Halloween or read *Sweet Valley High*, when my mother launched herself into one battle after another over my heart and mind. First there was a skirmish over evolution, then another over sex education, then a full-on war over the fact that my tenth-grade English teacher assigned the immoral novel *Chronicle of a Death Foretold* by Gabriel García Márquez.

I started making minor rebellions. At night I listened to *Loveline* with the volume down low. I hid racy books from the twenty-five-cent shelf at the used bookstore under my mattress. But I still followed the letter of the law. I never cursed. I never used the Lord's name in vain. I'd still never kissed anyone—maybe because no one seemed interested in kissing me. Meanwhile, week after week, those fat missives from Focus on the Family kept coming, filled with all the things that were still wrong with the world. I didn't keep up with them anymore. They piled up on the dining room table along with the unopened bills.

One Sunday my family drove to Baltimore for a dedication service for our sister church, which was finally trading their old storefront space for a custom-built megachurch in a safer, more suburban part of town. The service was an all-day affair with hours of choral performances, fire-and-brimstone sermons, and spontaneous bursts of prophecies, worship songs, and altar calls. The Spirit was running thick.

As hundreds of people swayed to the soft music of pianos and guitars, lifting their hands to the Lord and murmuring praise under their breath, a woman with a low, hoarse voice delivered a word over the church. She claimed that five years from that day, the congregation would triple in size and need to move yet again. The news traveled like electricity around that mauve sanctuary, and everyone around me squeezed their eyes closed and murmured their gratitude to God. Their voices rose again and I knew more prophecies were coming. But my right temple began to throb, and the sanctuary started to feel less like a temple and more like a cage. A refrain echoed and buzzed in my head: *None of this is true.*

I looked around and saw all those beaten-down mechanics and plumbers and carpenters, their wives shushing their babies, everyone trying to live like their lot was enough. They didn't seem particularly blessed by God, but still they tucked envelopes stuffed with cash into the offering plate and passed out quarters to their children, so no one would be empty-handed when the deacons passed the offering plate. I watched the boys my age, their skin pocked with acne, sneaking peeks at Pastor Jim's willowy daughters. Everyone came to church hoping for a lift, only to slump hours later when that charged feeling faded. In the middle of the fold were girls like Miss Kathy's daughter, who had preened and plucked herself into the vision of the virtuous woman, and on the outside were girls like Molly and Emmy, who had chosen the other path. But I didn't want to be either one. I stood up and slipped past the worshippers, slowly making my way to the ladies' room, where I sat on the toilet fully clothed and held my face in my hands.

It had been in a bathroom just like this that I had first felt the Spirit coming to me. When I received my prayer language, it felt like proof the Holy Spirit had X-rayed my life from up in heaven and called it good. It was my key to the kingdom, my guarantee that when the seventh trumpet sounded and Jesus returned in a cloud of glory, I'd be summoned up to meet the faithful. But now, four years later, I was ready to turn that key in. It had become too heavy. If I kept carrying it around, then I couldn't pick up anything else. So I sat there in the bathroom at that church in Baltimore and whispered to God that I was bowing out. To soften the blow and make it less terrifying, I told God I was taking a sabbatical from believing. A break. I'd probably be back, but for now I needed to go off on my own. And then I dug a ballpoint pen out of my white patent leather purse and scribbled a note on a torn scrap of paper.

November 5, 1995
Jessica Wilbanks is no longer a Christian.

For a long time I sat there staring at that slip of paper, horrified at my boldness, half expecting some earthquake or thunderbolt to rip me from my perch on the toilet. But all I heard was the dull hum of the heating system and a few stray voices coming in from the hall. The Holy Ghost had departed from me. No longer were there evil spirits lurking close by, to dive in at the slightest sign of trouble or joy, no angels watching from afar to offer protection. Now I was simply myself—a clump of cells directed by a series of synapses and neurons. I had a feeling that there would be no going back.

When I returned to the service with that talisman in my pocket, my heart was no longer soft and pliable. I stiffened up during the endless hymns, mouthing the words but refusing to let the melodies trickle into my marrow. I kept my eyes on the ground instead of closing them tightly during the final prayers. When we packed into the car for the long ride back to the county, I stared out the window and ignored my brothers' games in the backseat next to me. When my mother spoke to me, I felt like she was talking through a vast expanse of water. She didn't know me anymore. I was one of them, but at the same time I wasn't one of them. I felt as changed as if I had lost my virginity in that bathroom, or gunned someone down. It was just like Pastor Jim preached about in his sermons on free will. When God wrapped his salvation around you and sent the Holy Ghost to guide your path, it was up to you to decide to walk away. God won't stop you from slipping out from under his wing and trotting off into the world with only your thin skin to protect you.

Within a few weeks I found myself on the same beach I used to walk with my father and the twins. My friend Sophie, a transfer student at Calverton, finally agreed to let me tag along with her old friends from Calvert High as they partied on the beach. Someone handed me a can of Miller Lite and I popped the top open and took a long swig like it was something I did every day. The more I drank the looser the world seemed.

The sun went down over the top of the cliff and the air grew chilly. One of the boys made a fire from cast-off bits of driftwood and I pulled on a sweatshirt. A girl with kohl-lined eyes and long, tangled hair gave me a Camel Light. As she lit my cigarette I felt the soft pillow of her breasts against mine and my insides suddenly felt hollowed out. She was so much more beautiful than any of the acne-scarred boys throwing things into the fire. She and I talked softly and the night shrank around us. I felt like a different girl. Not the good girl, not the bookworm. I felt more like Molly and Emmy, swinging their feet from the brick wall at the middle school, taunting the world loudly and laughing when it answered back.

In another few years I'd be able to leave that town, with its endless acres of woods and miles of shoreline, cut through the middle by that one long ribbon of a highway. I'd need to be careful until then, covering my tracks. I'd be one girl on Sunday morning and another girl the rest of the week. At church I'd pretend to take notes during the sermon and no one would know I had stopped recording the pastor's words and had started writing down my own thoughts instead.

Chapter 6

Ori and Joe

When my friend's mother pulled into my parents' driveway, the sun already lay low on the tree line, infusing the cornfields that surrounded the house with a thick, yellow light. It was the September of my senior year, and I flounced into the house in my too-short plaid uniform skirt and knee socks and threw my bookbag on the dining room table. My mother fussed with the ever-expanding pile of dishes by the sink, and my father sat reading a newspaper at the blond wood table in the middle of the room, wearing a polo shirt stamped with the name "The King's Masons," an all-Christian masonry crew he had worked with years before. It was strange that he was home so early on a day when it wasn't raining. He cut his eyes at me over his bifocals and I made a face at him and snagged an apple from the bowl of fruit on the table. But when I tried to tell my parents about what my physics teacher had done that day, my father kept his eyes on the paper and my mother didn't turn around, just kept fiddling with the dishes. I trailed off and they didn't seem to notice.

"Hello?" I said, not looking up at first, still focused on peeling the skin off the apple. When I looked up, my father was standing in front of me with his mouth open, clearing his throat and shifting around. My mother was drying her hands on a dishtowel.

"Your father and I want to talk to you." Her voice was strange and raspy, and I started to sit down at the table.

"Not here. Outside."

"Mom, what's going on?"

"Leave the apple," she said.

As I followed them out to the yard, my first thought was that someone had died. But I could hear my brothers wrestling in the living room, five-year-old Joshua acting as a referee. It must have been my dad's mother, I thought.

We walked out into the chilly September evening. Our new rented farmhouse was white with red shutters, a brick-red chimney, and a long, wide front porch. Sixty yards out in the middle of that green ocean of a yard were three lawn chairs, the cheap kind with rusted metal legs and plastic canvas plaits. One for my mother, one for my father, and one for me. When I saw those chairs, I decided that the years of my father's temper and my mother's sadness had caught up with them and they had finally decided to get a divorce. I prepared myself, wondering where my dad would live and who would cook dinner for him.

My mother still held a blue-and-white checkered dishtowel in her lap. She started speaking, her voice quivering. She usually stuttered when she was nervous, but the words came out clean and plain.

She said, "We know that you are a homosexual. Your father read your journal."

The soft noise of the crickets and cicadas in the background turned into an overpowering buzz that drowned out my mother's voice and whatever my father said after that. Some duller, more primitive part of my mind unpacked their words and pieced the story together. Their discovery had come several weeks before. I'd spent a Friday night at a friend's house, staying up until dawn watching *Escape from the Blue Lagoon* and music videos, raiding her parents' refrigerator for chips and drinking Mountain Dew. Back at the farmhouse my father was up late too, reading one of his Westerns in my bed. That wasn't unusual—for as long as I can remember he slept on the couch, passing out in the early evening with a couch pillow behind his head and no blanket, his belly rising and falling, snorting and shaking with his breath. When an empty bed was available, he took advantage of it.

My father's story was that he had dropped his book behind my bed. When he reached for it he'd picked up instead the lime-green spiral notebook that I had squirreled away by the headboard and in which I wrote about the days remaining until I left for college and all the things I wanted. He'd opened it and followed the purple curlicues of my adolescent handwriting and learned what I'd been up to. I hadn't held anything back, not to that notebook. I had written about going out deep into the cornfield and bringing along a smashed pack of cigarettes and a pack of gas station matches nabbed from the junk drawer. I had written about that night at the beach a few years before, when I felt a tug of desire for the girl with kohl-rimmed eyes and tangled hair. I had written about smoking pot from a smelly old foil pipe with friends at the beach near my aunt's house.

But worst of all I had written about kissing my friend Sophie in my parents' living room during a sleepover a month before. Sophie didn't fit in with the rest of the crowd at Calverton. She listened to Janis Joplin and Bob Dylan and still hung out with her old friends from Calvert High on the weekends. She couldn't have been more different than my white-bread friends who loved boy bands and pop music. Sophie seemed to be in tune with something bigger, something I thought I was moving toward.

My notebook told the story about how, one night, when Sophie was sleeping over on the futon on the living room floor, she played that girls' game of having a secret she wouldn't tell, and for hours I cajoled her and tried to talk her into confessing. She wouldn't say anything. Finally, she admitted that she had a crush on someone, that she stayed up late thinking of what it would be like to kiss this person. I finally realized that she was talking about me, but I didn't let on that I knew. We kept chatting and teasing and meanwhile my heart was racing. She took my face in her hands and kissed me softly, and suddenly I was all body and no mind at all. As I felt her lips against mine, my brain started up with all the reasons this was wrong and unnatural. But it was dark and quiet and her skin was so soft that part of me felt like it would smear if I touched it. Her mouth tasted faintly of raspberries, and after a few moments my mind turned off. In the morning, when I woke up to her brown hair splayed out on the pillow beside me I felt no guilt at all, only an incredible sense of lightness. I felt older and wiser, more confident. A woman. As we ate scrambled eggs and pancakes to the sound of my brothers' shrieks, I gazed at her across the table and we smiled secret smiles at each other.

There is a particular kind of feeling that tattoos itself into your bones, where it aches for days and weeks afterward, and keeps aching whenever you think of it years later. Out there on that autumn night on the lawn, as the sky went blue-black and the seagulls made their way over the corn and toward their nests, I felt myself slipping away. My parents built a tower of words, *I don't know you anymore* and *evil* and *sin* and *unnatural.* But I wasn't listening. I knew that story. I'd heard it a thousand times, from Pastor Jim's lips, from Miss Kathy, from my mother's books about how a Christian ought to live. I knew about that great force of evil in the world that warped men and women's natural passions for one another and turned them inside out. It was the story of an abomination, an evil as powerful and insidious as a poisonous gas. I had heard that story in my head the moment I drew back from kissing Sophie, and again when I washed my face and hands in the bathroom. But there was another voice in there too, a voice that said what we did was gentle and innocent and nothing to feel shame over.

My mother was shocked and sad. She couldn't put it together; she just didn't understand. But my father inspected his nails and then looked at me coolly. He had tasted more of what the world had to offer than my mother had. He wasn't surprised that I had said yes to cigarettes and alcohol, warm arms and lips, female or male. But they both rejected the idea that I was intrinsically bad. Instead they had decided that evil had gotten into me and jumped under my skin. This unnatural sexual urge that I had was a virus, a pollutant. It went without saying that I would never be allowed to spend time with Sophie again.

Sitting there, hearing my parents' words wash over me, I felt the dull burn of a brand across my chest. *Homosexual.* There had been a nest and I had fallen out of it. I already knew there was no going back inside. As night stretched over the lawn my parents studied me as if I was an intractable algebra problem. They couldn't solve for X; they couldn't figure out what had gone so wrong. It would have been different if I had reached for a boy, or even a man. Those desires were a well-trodden path, mistakes thousands of girls before me had made. But I hadn't picked the apple. I had reached for the snake itself.

※

When it was over I walked up the stairs to my room and cried until I seemed empty of everything. When the tears finally stopped my mind went through the options. I could hitchhike to DC, pay forty dollars for a bus ticket and be in a new city by morning. Or I could stay and find a way to make it through the year. I had already made a list of colleges to apply to and would take the SAT again in a few months. I was so close to the life I had dreamed of. What was one year, I thought to myself. Anyone could get through a year.

After that I began treating myself and my desires like a feral animal, something to be chained down in a dark stall and tamed through discipline. I built a fortress around myself, slipping into a new group of friends and ignoring Sophie's confused stares. That year held a bright kind of darkness. I spent all my time outside of school tucked away in my bedroom, scrawling fragments of poems in my notebooks, feeding my wild feelings with rock music piped off the radio and paperback novels I borrowed from the library. My room was small and had two windows, and out of both you could see the endless ocean of corn, green in the spring and curled up on itself in the fall, a rustling, crackling field of straw.

When I came home from school every day at four o'clock I looked for my mother's car, and if it wasn't there, I ran upstairs and ripped off my button-down shirt and plaid skirt, then pulled on a pair of jean shorts and a tank top. I grabbed the cigarettes and matches I'd hidden under the sweaters in the top shelf of the closet. When I left the house I could hear the screen door banging behind me and my brothers calling, but I didn't stop until I threaded my way through the cornstalks behind the house, tiptoeing so as not to bend the stalks and leave signs for my brothers to track me down.

When I got far enough back and the stalks waved higher than my head and it seemed like there was no way for anyone to find me, I struck match after match, using my shirt as a tent until I got the first of those cigarettes to light. When it finally caught fire, I stomped some of the cornstalks down to make a bed for myself there in the field. The smell of tobacco flooded over my body like a promise of the cities I wanted to be in so badly.

The nights were the hardest. I felt so alone, lying in bed in the dark, and found myself wanting desperately to pray. I didn't believe in God anymore, but my faith was like a faucet with broken handles. It kept coming in gushes and I couldn't seem to turn it off. I needed a hand to hold on the other side of belief. And so I did something people have been doing for centuries—I made up my own God, the God I needed at that particular moment. I peeled the shell off the gruff, bearded God I had always been taught to worship and gave him a new name and a new face. I couldn't decide whether this new God should be a man or a woman, so I decided in favor of both. The woman I named Oriana—I don't even know where I got that name from—Ori for short. She was dark and strong with muscular arms and plain, masculine clothes. She was impatient and fierce, wise and righteously angry. The man sitting next to her, Joe, was more of a boy or an elf than a man. He was infinitely loving and patient. Maternal without being suffocating, tender without being maudlin. Unlike the God I had grown up with, these two were located in real physical space, in the landscape that was more beautiful to me than any other place in the world—the estuaries of the Chesapeake Bay.

In my mind I placed them on a large, dark-green corduroy couch, and I placed that couch in the Chesapeake Bay. There was a sandbar off the beach near our house—one that came up suddenly, two hundred yards from shore. You had to go into the water waist-deep to get to it, and once there, you could lie on your back, and at the right time of the day the water wouldn't even touch your chest. So it was there that I placed my new divinities—sprawled out on that couch in divine ennui, Ori on the left and Joe on the right, and there they watched my life unfold on the enormous sky before them.

In my days of fervent belief, I used to call out to God in fragments—in joy or sadness—God, my math test. God, my brother's broken leg. God, the rent money. And sometimes in praise: God, the way our black lab followed me patiently as I walked on the beach. God, the green of the corn. During my senior year my prayers shifted only slightly. "Ori and Joe," I prayed, "let me get into college." "Ori and Joe, let me get out of this place." From their couch in the water Ori and Joe shook their heads at my choices and encouraged me when I did something hard. Whenever my mother's gaze landed on me and her eyes narrowed, I retreated to that sandbar in which there was total acceptance. Ori was looking at me with unconditional love and support, she was strong and not scared. But Joe was crying—he knew how much this hurt me. They were the rope I held onto as I tried to make it out of my parents' house and into my own life. For years I worshipped my new gods, secretly and privately. I prayed to my new gods in litany form, next to poems I'd copied from the *Norton Anthology of World Literature* and my own rough attempts at stories. I called out to them in my notebooks, in red pen and black and blue. They never answered me, but I reminded myself that God hadn't really seemed to answer either.

❧

That summer I tagged along with my father when he drove into Northern Virginia on Saturdays. I rode the Metro into Washington, DC, and got off at random stops to walk around. With a Metro card in my pocket I felt free, the same clear, exhilarating feeling I used to have when I got up before dawn with my father to walk Calvert Beach with the twins. The day stretched out like a horizon in front of me and all that time was mine. There were no brothers around to distract me, no mother to read over my shoulder, no father to come home with darting eyes and make everyone tremble. I spent hours in the Smithsonian museums, gaping at abstract paintings and reconstructed dinosaur bones. I bought egg rolls in Chinatown and walked all the way up to Dupont Circle to eat gummy bears on a bench in front of a marble fountain with a statue of a naked woman. I talked to everyone: store clerks, security guards, the homeless people who set up their tents on the sidewalks of the city. Wherever

I went, I kept my eyes open for the city of sin Pastor Jim talked about, but I couldn't find it.

One day I steeled myself and walked into the gay and lesbian bookstore on Connecticut Avenue. Two rainbow flags framed the doorway. The man behind the register had a shock of grey hair and wore thick black-rimmed glasses. He looked like one of the deacons at church and didn't pay me any attention. I wandered through the aisles and trained my eyes on the sides of the books. I was afraid to pick them up, but the titles alone were an education. A woman appeared, friendly, with a masculine edge to her. Her face was kind, but hard at the same time, so different from the women at church, with their old-fashioned hairstyles.

"Is there anything I can help you with?"

I peered up at her and was immediately tongue-tied. I wanted to ask her if she grew up like me, listening to sermon after sermon about how she herself was an abomination, and what it had taken to get those words out of her head. If sometimes she got so nervous she bit down on the skin on the inside of her cheeks or the skin on the top of her knuckles. If she and I and that bespectacled man behind the counter and all those young men in tight jeans hanging out over by the fountain were going to hell. I wanted to ask her what it was about us that scared people so badly. Where it was that I could hide my notebooks to keep my parents from finding them. If I should even bother coming home for Christmas when I got to college. Why my heart leapt for Sophie at the same time it sometimes leapt for boys. If there was some sign that women can wear to show they're interested in each other. A pinky ring, a green scarf?

The chime on the door clanged and her eyes darted over to see who had just walked in. When she met my eyes again,

I told her I was just browsing. On the way out, I picked up a copy of the *Washington Blade*, and on the subway I splayed it open on my legs so nobody could see what I was reading. I read articles about AIDS, a group called PFLAG, a profile of some C-list actress, a review of *Angels in America*. As the train tunneled underneath the Potomac I read the singles ads, amazed by everything people wanted to do to each other. I was too nervous to bring the newspaper home, even tucked in my bag, so I threw it away in the garbage can at the King Street Metro station.

The cab of my father's ancient pickup truck smelled like engine oil and lawn clippings, and I had to be careful not to catch my jean skirt on the wire poking out of the ripped seat. When we crossed the Woodrow Wilson Bridge, I looked down and saw that the newsprint had stained the skin above my knee red and black. I licked my fingers and rubbed the words away.

۞

Somehow I made it through that final year of high school, and when the day of my departure finally came, my father drove me to college in a Ford F150 with a stuck passenger-side door and windows that wouldn't roll up. He hadn't finished college himself and didn't think it had done much for the clients he laid brick for, but he was always up for an adventure. As we were leaving, my mother pressed a series of plastic shopping bags into my hands. One was filled with a sack lunch for us to eat on the way, another was full of tiny wrapped presents for me to open once I arrived at school. She also pressed on me various books, blankets, a calling card, and my favorite plate, which I was too ashamed to refuse to take. She cried when I left and I felt something swell in my throat. I said goodbye to Obere and Sam, who at sixteen and twelve were already starting to push against my father's rules. When I hugged Joshua goodbye, he wept with the savage love of a five-year-old, pummeled me with his tiny fists, and then ran to hide in my mother's bedroom. My father threw my suitcases in the back of the truck and we set off. As we drove, the woods turned into fields and the white light of morning faded, turning the sky bright blue.

The truck hummed over the long bridge that spanned the Susquehanna River and then climbed up through Pennsylvania and New Jersey, crossing the Hudson River at the Tappan Zee Bridge. On the way my father told me all of his stories, most of them for the fifth or sixth time. Stories about things he had done before he had given his life to the Lord. Hiking through the woods that lined the reservoirs in Washington State, fishing in Alaska, playing football in high school in Virginia, serving in Vietnam, living in a rundown tobacco barn in Maryland just before he married my mom. Those stories had been my first introduction to the larger world, but now I couldn't wait for them to be over. I let him go on and on, and while he talked I watched the landscape go by, letting his stories fade out the open windows.

Hampshire College sat in the Pioneer Valley of Western Massachusetts, between the Berkshire mountains to the west and the hills around the Quabbin Reservoir to the east. We drove through the night, and when we finally made it to that tiny town where I'd spend my college years, dawn was breaking in a smoky haze over the fields and farms. The wooden houses seemed like toy houses, and there were huge sycamores in the yards, the leaves burning with a purple fire. We were both speechless at the beauty of it. My father maneuvered that ancient pickup between all the Subarus and

Volvos parked haphazardly in the quad. We lugged suitcases and garbage bags into my new dorm room. I didn't think I'd ever be coming home again, so I'd brought everything that mattered with me: snapshots I'd snatched out of my father's photo albums of my brothers and me when we were young, clothes for warm and cool weather, boxes of paperback books with cracked spines.

The other parents lingered on benches outside and in hallways, the men with carefully trimmed beards, tweed jackets, and heavy gold watches around their wrists. Some of their daughters had shaved hair and wore men's clothes, and some of the boys had the build and walk of women. My father clammed up, tucking in his faded polo shirt, brushing at the mortar dust stains. I asked him if he wanted to get dinner, but he shook his head and said he had to get on the road. I was relieved, and wrapped my arms around him like I was hugging him for the last time. His beard was rough on my cheek and there was a sour smell of chewing tobacco on his breath. For the first time in years it felt like I was home and he was on the periphery. That feeling delighted me and saddened me at the same time, and then I turned around to go upstairs to my dorm room. I didn't think about him again for weeks.

Chapter 7

Mushrooms

Just before we left campus Bethany showed me a trick. She scrunched up the sandwich-sized baggie of dusty mushroom caps and stems in her slender fingers, then she looped an elastic ponytail holder around it several times, until it was a little smaller than a golf ball. She put it inside a fake can of Sprite that screwed open at the top, then tucked the can into a brown paper bag beside her guitar in the trunk of her Saturn. She explained that all of that was probably enough for our purposes—a three-hour drive north from Western Massachusetts to Vermont—but if we'd been going any farther we'd have had to hide the plastic bag in a jar of peanut butter.

I drew heavily on my snow-damp cigarette, then looked away so as not to encourage her. God only knew where she had gotten that can from. I would've just stuck the mushrooms under the owner's manual in the glove compartment and hoped for the best. Or more likely I'd have never left campus in the first place. My idea of fun was smaller than hers, but then again, I'd seen less. Bethany had grown up in a three-thousand-square-foot mansion she called The Palace.

Her father owned a trucking company and had the same easy way with Teamsters that he had with accountants and city councilmen. She'd inherited his quick smile and confident way of walking through the world, and I was dependent on her for everything, from explaining movie references to loaning me the sweaters I hadn't realized I needed to make it through the Massachusetts winter. I was wearing one of her sweaters right now. It was lovely—mohair, rose-colored, and soft as a lamb, but it wasn't enough to keep me warm.

The snow fell on the icy parking lot in feathery clumps the size of mothballs that left wet splotches on my coat and soaked my green-striped wool mittens. I was willing to hear about the peanut butter trick, but learning techniques for eluding drug dogs weren't my highest priority at that moment. Instead I wanted to get in the car and turn the heat on full-blast. I stomped my feet and blew on my fingers through my mittens, but Bethany ignored me and rummaged through the pockets of her down coat, looking for her lighter. I sighed but didn't say a word. It was eleven and we were supposed to have left at nine-thirty to beat the blizzard, but then Bethany needed to run to the store for cigarettes and when we got there I realized I'd forgotten my wallet, and then Lauren had to run back to Tom's dorm to get the guitar capo she'd loaned him. We'd crisscrossed campus three times already and I was frozen to the bone.

It was Saturday night and the air was already getting that electric feel that came over the campus when hundreds of carefully attended-to bodies came out of hiding to gather in little pockets in various corners of the quad. Even from the parking lot we could hear the peals of laughter as people decided whether to start the night at the parties in Prescott or the ones in Enfield. On any other night Bethany, Lauren, and I would be in the middle of all of it, clutching bottles of cheap beer that Bethany's boyfriend had procured for us at the liquor store down the street, batting our sticky, mascaraed eyelashes at each other, and trying to decide if we'd start the night at the party in Enfield or stay in Prescott to smoke a joint with my roommates. Not that it really mattered. The parties in Prescott were lit by disco balls and the ones in Enfield were more likely to feature a Grateful Dead cover band, but wherever we ended up, things would go the same way. We'd dance for a while and then someone would pass around an ashy one-hitter and we'd take deep drags long after it was kicked. We'd grab a red plastic cup and pump the keg until the foam cleared and a lukewarm splash of Natty Ice hiccupped up through the tube. When things got boring inside we'd go outside to share a cigarette and start looking around. But tonight was different. Bethany not only tracked down an eighth of mushrooms but also the perfect place to do them: a tiny cabin in the woods of rural Vermont. It would be the first time we'd ventured off the Western Massachusetts campus for an overnight adventure, the first time we'd said no to the campus parties and hit the road on our own.

When Lauren finally showed up with the capo, Bethany put on a CD and drove north. I curled up in the back of the car with all the bedding, keeping a close eye on Lauren's cigarette butt to make sure the ash didn't blow back into the window and land on me. I couldn't make out the conversation in the front seat over the music or see anything out the window thanks to the snow, so instead I rested my forehead on the icy window and chewed the skin inside my cheek, trying to calm myself.

I shivered and asked Bethany to turn the heat up a little, and then I tried to imagine what my family was doing now back in Maryland. Earlier that day I'd dodged a call from my mother, trying to get out the door on time. Now she was probably up late, reading *Woman's Day* in bed and eating a Hershey bar, enjoying the few hours a day that she had to herself. My dad would be passed out shirtless on the couch, snoring away as a John Wayne movie flickered on the TV, a throw pillow balled up under one arm and a half-empty bowl of popcorn on the floor by his shoes. Joshua would be fast asleep upstairs in the middle of a nest of stuffed animals, his arms up behind his head in that helpless way that kids slept. Sam would have stuffed a towel under his bedroom door to block the light so my mom wouldn't know he was up late playing Sega. But when I got to Obere I came up blank. He was sixteen now and I didn't know what he did on a Saturday night.

♯

When we finally got to the cabin, Bethany brought out her guitar and she and Lauren ran through their usual set of ballads: Ani DiFranco, Tori Amos, and Stevie Nicks. I summoned up the courage to chime in on the harmonies with a wavering, off-tune soprano, adding the slightest shadow to their melody. Patrick nodded his head to the beat and stared too long at Lauren as she sang. To my eighteen-year-old self he seemed middle-aged and established, with a house of his own, but he was probably only in his late twenties or early thirties, an itinerant ski bum who had rented the old cabin for a few hundred bucks.

When the singing was over we drank off-brand vodka with Sprite and Bethany and Patrick tried to explain what the mushrooms would feel like when they came on, but they ended up just telling stories of previous mushroom trips, stories that were confusing and circular and did nothing to prepare us for what was to come. Eventually Bethany made us open-faced peanut butter sandwiches with mushroom caps on them, carefully splitting up the stems into four equal shares.

While we waited for the mushrooms to kick in Patrick dumped logs on the fire, but they were damp from the snow and quickly smothered the coals. His face reddened and he gulped his beer faster, nagging Lauren to play something else. She didn't answer, just sat staring at the fire like it was a fascinating and mystical place. I was used to living out my nights in a buttery haze of drunkenness, and I poured heavily to hasten it on, but it didn't come. Instead I felt hyperconscious of the way I was sitting and couldn't get comfortable. Bethany told stories about her adventures in New Jersey as a teenager, playing in a Tool cover band, falling asleep hugging a grown man on the back of a motorcycle, and then Lauren picked up the guitar again and Bethany started singing. She and Patrick talked for a while after that, and Lauren and I listened wide-eyed, our eyes on the fire, not trusting our voices.

After a few hours, Bethany stretched and announced that she was tired. Lauren and I peered at each other and then yawned theatrically and followed her up to the loft bedroom. Bethany hunted around in her duffel bag, looking for her toothbrush, and I managed to make my way to the single bed in the corner of the room. I lay down and tried to get my bearings, but the cracks in the shiplap beside me contracted and expanded, growing wider. I looked over at Bethany and Lauren settling into the double bed across the room. They seemed to be talking, but I couldn't hear them. The dark feeling that had come over me in the car came crashing back, and I felt my throat constricting. At that moment either Bethany or Lauren must have flipped the light switch off, leaving me in sudden and complete darkness. In an instant the world turned over. My mind went fuzzy and I was convinced I had gone blind, but I was too terrified to call out to anyone. I felt myself teetering on the edge of a vortex and I didn't know how to get out of it. My mind lost its hold on solidity and became a mishmash of shapes and sounds and feelings. I was stuck in the middle of a dark wood on a cold night, and there was no way of getting back to the light.

Somewhere in that mess and swarm, I remembered my mother telling me about the gift of tongues. She didn't talk about that language the same way our pastor did, but instead told me that the gift of tongues was meant for a time when you needed God's love and mercy but you didn't know how to ask for it. She told me about a time when she felt like she was losing her grip on her family and her faith, when she needed God desperately but was too terrified and upset to ask him for anything. She said she had called out to God in tongues, and he heard her prayer. She promised that if I was ever at loose ends, I could open my mouth and God himself would hear me and come to my aid. I knew those tongues were still deep inside me somewhere. I just had to wake them up.

On the strength of my mother's secondhand promise, I rested my damp, sweaty cheek against the pillow and opened my mouth. From deep inside my throat those whispered tongues climbed out, and I cried out to God in the language of my childhood, asking that my sight be given back to me, asking to be kept safe from the maze that had become my mind. I wept silently and told God I was sorry for everything, sorry for the sin and the separation, sorry for my pride and my arrogance, sorry for lusting after sensation. In that moment I meant every word. The darkness subsided, and I could just begin to make out the dark shadow of the tall pines outside the window and the red blur of an alarm clock on the bedside table. I wasn't blind after all. My breathing evened out and my heart stopped racing. It was a miracle of New Testament caliber, water to wine. The world seemed good again. I thought I might be able to be good again. I nuzzled into my pillow and felt my eyelids closing. Within minutes I was sleeping the bottomless sleep of a child.

§

The next morning there was a damp spot on my pillow and a sore nub high in the back of my throat. I tiptoed out of bed and stretched, watching the sunlight from the dusty single-pane windows catch on the raw boards of the wall behind the bed. When I remembered the night before a blade of shame wrenched into my belly.

Bethany showed up in the doorway in a too-big T-shirt, her hair piled into a bun on the top of her head. She winked at me. "Hey, sleepyhead. Sorry about last night. I don't know why I got so tired. Maybe I'm getting my period. Want a mimosa? Patrick's making them."

I nodded. "Be down in a second."

The water trickling down from the clogged-up showerhead felt like it had been pumped straight up from some ice-covered river. I stood rigid in the shower stall and held my breath as it flattened my hair and poured over my goose-pimpled back. The pure cold shattered any mystical sensibilities leftover from the night before. I started working my shivering fingers through my tangled hair, washing out the smoke and sweat until the skin on the pads of my fingers pruned up. In the kitchen a mimosa was waiting for me, maybe even some toast. I'd feel better when I got some food in my belly. I clenched my eyes closed and ducked back under the water, then reached for the tap and dried myself off gingerly with a crusty hand towel. Bethany's raucous laugh echoed through the drywall from the kitchen downstairs, and Lauren said something in a peevish tone. There was a tube of gel on the counter next to a pink toothbrush, probably Bethany's. I worked the gel through my hair and set my face, narrowing my eyes and sucking my cheeks in, then eyed myself in the fogged-up mirror. With my wet hair plastered to my head I looked big-eyed and vulnerable, more like a child than a woman.

"Grow up," I whispered to my reflection. I had made my choice. That long-ago day in the bathroom of a church in Baltimore, I'd traded safety and security for freedom and set off into the world alone. I was no longer a child of God, no longer one of the chosen. It wasn't fair for me to deny God in the daylight and then when night came, beg the Holy Spirit to swoop down and rescue me. It was time to stop mourning for what used to be.

Downstairs the sickly-sweet smell of pot hung over the living room like a cloud. I heard Bethany's laugh again, tinkling softly over the whistle of a teakettle. I steeled my shoulders and walked into the room. This was the world I lived in now, a world in which nothing was sacred and nothing was damned, a world I had chosen for myself. I wanted to love it, but I didn't love it yet.

🌿 *Chapter 8* 🌿

Live Nativity

I called my mother from my dorm room, J-307, and she answered in a breathy Southern lilt. When she heard me on the line her voice jumped an octave. Somewhere in the world my heart still pumped blood into my body. I had not been snatched away by some malevolent man while walking home from the library at midnight. The world had not yet swept me into its trap. She breathed my nickname, *Tootie*, the only name my family has ever called me, and the sheer pleasure in her voice got the old anxiety machine going in my brain, so loudly I could hardly hear her over the panicked whine of its motor.

I could almost see my mother there in the tiny living room of my parents' new rental house deep in the woods. She'd be straightening her shoulders and putting down the broom, shushing my bellowing father, winding the tangled phone line through the screen door to the porch, where she could have some privacy. She'd push the cats off the worn-down wicker loveseat that overlooked that expanse of farmland, and brush the willow leaves from the cushion.

She barraged me with questions and I answered brightly, at first, leaving out the grimier details of my life, smoothing over the pieces that didn't fit the story I wanted to tell her. I told her I was having fun with my friends, but didn't tell her how I'd been up until 4 a.m. the night before chugging down syrupy vodka-based concoctions with the homeless kid from Brooklyn who was squatting in the double room across the hall. I told her I was meeting nice people, but didn't elaborate about my current campaign to seduce the skater-punk waitress at Packard's sports bar. I told her my courses were going well, but I didn't tell her I'd been sleeping through my 10 a.m. classes and my papers were already weeks late. She asked me how the food was, and I hedged. I told her I couldn't afford a meal plan, not on the ten hours a week that I was allocated through the work-study program.

She asked me if I had enough money and I hedged again. My job at the library kept me in cigarettes and Bethany was generous with booze, but every week I racked up more and more debt at the campus store. My mother didn't ask about my schoolwork, so I didn't tell her about the classes I'd picked at random—Feminist Fictions, Anthropological Approaches to Popular Culture, Ever Since Darwin, and Human Memory—or my latest obsessions, the cart-wheeling philosophy of Julia Kristeva and the poetry of Rainer Maria Rilke. Instead, when it was my turn to talk I asked the same open-air questions that she'd asked, "How's the family? How's work?" She told me that my uncle's latest attempt to quit drinking seemed to have stuck, though my father tried to talk him out of it, telling him life was too short to cut out what makes you happiest. "That man!" she sighed.

My mother told me how she'd gone back to work for the first time in eighteen years, manning the phones at Catholic

Charities and helping the social workers rustle up resources for people who couldn't make it from payday to payday. She said my dad was hurting for work. He'd only had a handful of jobs since the beginning of winter, so they needed to come up with a plan.

"We'll figure it out," she said. "We always do." I perched on my bed and lit another cigarette. "Here's your dad."

My father coughed and cleared his throat, answering in monosyllables as I ran through my usual series of questions. If we'd been sitting on the porch drinking coffee together he'd be full of stories, but he tended to clam up on the phone. I tried to think of something to amuse him and ended up recounting the plot of the new Leonardo DiCaprio movie.

"Is that right," he said flatly, and a minute later my mother got back on the phone. She told me how the landlord had gotten into it with Dad about the old cars that had been put out to pasture in the backyard. And now it looked like my dad's truck would join them soon—the engine was probably shot. She said the dog had gotten caught in a fox trap and had a limp for a while but now he was his old self again.

"What else?" she mused. "We don't see too much of your brother Obere. He spends all his time with his new girlfriend. But Lord knows I can't talk to your father about that." Underneath her flippant tone I heard a certain octave that told me there was another story she wasn't telling.

I asked about my brothers and my mother told me about Joshua's antics. I asked about my dad's health. I asked about Obere and Sam and my mother's voice finally lowered. Obere wasn't doing great. When he did come home, all he and Dad did was fight. And she had caught Sam with marijuana again—peeled back a poster on his wall and found a full-sized plant stuck in a hole in the wall. Last weekend, he and my father had come to blows, and my mother had called the police because it didn't look like either one was going to back down.

I felt my mind freeze up. My mother checked to make sure I was still on the phone. "Just thinking," I said. I tugged my window open with my hand and felt the frigid air pour into the room, raising goose bumps on my arms. A moment later the question came, forcibly light: "When are you coming home?"

"Soon," I said. "I'll be home soon." The holiday break was a few weeks away and a boy who had a crush on a friend of mine had promised me a ride back to Maryland.

"Let me pray for you," my mother said. I said okay. Her voice steeled up a bit, and she asked God to protect me and walk with me. I didn't close my eyes, just tucked the receiver against my ear and looked out the window. A laughing couple threw snowballs at each other in the quad. When I finally hung up the phone, longing and shame tightened around my stomach like a belt. I thought of something my father had told me last summer. Apparently he'd walked into the kitchen to make himself a plate of something and he found my mother crying near the sink. She was crying over me and my future, as she had before and would again. She could only guess at what made up my life, far away in New England, but she knew it wasn't the life she would have chosen for me. My father could be tender when he needed to be and he said he had calmed her down, poured her a glass of iced tea. When she was feeling better he asked her what she thought I'd do when I finished school. He said she fixed him with those ice-blue eyes of hers and said, "Well, I guess she'll come home and be one of us again."

The college I had chosen was only thirty years old and seemed more like a campground than a college. The handful of buildings that littered the campus had been molded out of thick slabs of concrete in a dense, brutalist style. There was no consistency to the curriculum—instead each professor offered classes on his or her special area of interest to a small handful of students. Most of the professors were aging socialists who had first joined the faculty in the seventies, when the revolution seemed imminent. Many of them were grandparents now, but they still showed up for the peace marches in the town square and coached every new group of freshmen through divestment proceedings and other acts of civil disobedience. I had never seen a protest before and was surprised to find that the mood of the student body seemed to rise and fall in response to events whole oceans away, in Israel and Palestine and West Africa, places I only knew from books. While I worked my shift at the campus library I watched the students waving signs and banners and chanting in the quad outside. I was amazed at their fervor. Who were they talking to, exactly? No one seemed to be paying attention.

That first year of college was the first time I really noticed that metallic coil of anxiety buried deep in my belly. Much later I would realize it had been there all along, from that morning I went to school for the first time in a too-big navy-blue cardigan sweater and white socks that bagged around my skinny ankles, climbing carefully onto the school bus with my Snoopy lunchbox in one hand and my shiny green backpack in the other. My mother waved nervously from the sidewalk with baby Sam in her arms as Obere stomped in the leaves near the curb.

Everything I encountered that day was a shock, from the brusque tone of the bus driver to the industrial smell of the shiny linoleum in the hallway to the baggy T-shirts the other girls wore with pictures of cartoon characters I didn't recognize. At recess I avoided the packs of other kids and stayed close to my teacher's skirt, and when the bus pulled up beside our small white A-frame house that afternoon I couldn't get into my mother's arms fast enough. It had been such a shock to venture outside the tight confines of our house and find another world there, one with a different set of rules. Every day I had to leave that house where everything happened and go wait for a bus to come and scoop me up and take me away. I didn't want to go. I wanted to stay in that warm house with my mother and father and brothers for the rest of my life.

Both back then and now I felt so untethered. I had thought I'd had a grip on things, but it turned out I didn't know anything at all. I had never been so free in my life as I was in college, but now that freedom seemed so large and dark and hollow that it made me dizzy. The sheer weight of all that possibility thrummed in my head and made my stomach seize up. I tried to mother myself, chasing after health and wholeness like a dog chases a cat. Every night I wrote out a series of ambitious resolutions in my spiral-bound notebook. From now on I'd wake up at six every morning and walk over to the rec center to log thirty minutes on the treadmill. I'd take the bus to the supermarket and stock up on oatmeal and bagels and carrot sticks. I'd reserve a carrel on the third floor of the library and spend my evenings and weekends there, catching up on my assignments and getting ahead on my reading. I'd start calling my parents every Sunday and send Joshua a postcard once a week.

It was so clear to me what needed to be done, but after a while I stopped kidding myself. Things always went the same way despite my efforts. I stayed up all night reading some pulpy novel and then slept for most of the morning, and when I woke up I made instant coffee instead of eating breakfast. As the days got shorter and colder I withdrew from my friends and spent long nights curled up under my comforter in my dorm room, chain-smoking. Sometimes I'd sift through the old family photos I'd taken from my father's scrapbooks.

My favorite hours of the week were the ones I spent in my feminist literature class, gathered around a long blond-wood table discussing Margaret Atwood, Dorothy Allison, and Jeanette Winterson. I already owned most of the novels the professor assigned, but I'd never talked to anyone else about them. Our professor was a thin woman with a shock of coarse, gray hair who looked more like a midwife or a farmer than a professor. She had a long series of Ivy League degrees to her credit, but she encouraged us to call her by her first name, Jane. Unlike my teachers in high school, she seemed genuinely intrigued by her students. She urged us to draw on our own experiences in class discussions and the short essays we wrote in response to the books she assigned. Just before the holiday break, I wrote a long essay about my mother in response to a book we'd read by Doris Lessing. The piece revolved around my conflicted response to her piety and the guilt I felt about leaving my faith and my family behind me. A few days later, when we gathered in Emily Dickinson Hall around that long seminar table, my professor read a few of the essays out loud, mine among them. My classmates listened attentively and appreciatively, but I felt unsettled. It felt so strange to sit among my classmates and hear my family being conjured up in Jane's patrician accent, pinned into stark relief and frozen under the gaze of a room full of eighteen-year-olds.

A few days later in office hours, Jane smiled at me as if I was a rare specimen of bird. She told me that she didn't see many students who had made the leap that I had, who had been brave enough to trade in their old worldview for a new one. She said she was proud of me for my courage and wanted to hear more about my mother, my father, my brothers, and my hometown. I found myself offering up their stories—telling Jane how my mother had a college degree and used to be a vice president at a small research company. But when she got pregnant with me she quit her job and stayed home. Jane's eyes glowed as I talked, and I started to feel uncomfortable, like I was betraying some confidence. But she urged me on. I told her about growing up in the church, marching next to my brothers at the March for Life, watching my mother testify against the presence of witches in the public school curriculum.

Finally I told Jane that I had to go—I was late for my shift at the library. I was already halfway out the door when she called my name and asked me what I was planning to do after graduation. I knew then that I only had to say the word and she'd take me under her wing. I could tell her I wanted to be a writer, and she'd spell out the mysterious algorithms that led to agents and book contracts. I could tell her I wanted to study literature, and she'd pile up my arms with academic journals and books by obscure theorists. I could tell her I didn't know yet, and she'd tell me to come back for office hours next week and we'd talk about it more.

Instead an obstinate spirit rose up within me, and I found myself breezily saying that I hadn't really thought about it. I told her I'd probably move back home, get married, and have some kids. I don't know why I said it. Probably just to see her face flush with indignation.

A few weeks later, in my end-of-term course evaluation, Jane praised my writing, saying that the portrait of my mother conveyed a dire sense of doom, an inevitable feeling that what had been passed on to me, I would no doubt pass on to my own children. I was confused by that last line, so I dug through a stack of papers on my desk until I found the essay she'd been talking about. I perched on my bed and read it one more time. Now that I was looking for it, I could see what she meant. I couldn't put my finger on it exactly, but there was an ominous feeling somewhere between the lines.

I caught a ride back to Maryland with a second-year student who lived on the next hall over, a tall, arrogant guy named Corey with a permanent smirk and a small scar on his cheekbone. I curled up in the back seat and tried to sleep against the window while in the front seat Corey and his friend Ben argued about politics. Just outside Baltimore I woke up to find Ben driving far below the speed limit. When I peered out the window all I saw was a curtain of snowflakes. Ben and Corey sat on the edge of their seats, squinting into the flurry as the wipers did their best to keep the snow at bay. As it got darker and colder, more and more cars pulled over on the highway in an attempt to wait out the storm. We talked it through but decided to push on. After all, my father was waiting for us at a gas station off Suitland Parkway and there was no way of getting through to him to tell him we'd be even later than we were already.

Just before the exit for Baltimore, the car skidded on black ice, and the momentum sent us into a tailspin. The car spun around in a full circle, finally coming to a stop sideways across the highway. For a moment we were all speechless, motionless, and then finally Ben shook himself off and steered the car the right way around. No one said what we were all thinking—how differently things could have gone if there had been another car behind us.

By the time we reached the gas station, my father had been waiting for hours. My heart leapt when I spotted his rusty pickup truck idling near the phone booth. He put his arm around me and shook hands with Corey and Ben, wincing and shaking his head at the story of our near miss, then he hoisted my suitcase into the back of the truck and bungeed a tarp around it to protect it from the snow. On the long road back home I told him all about my friends and my classes, breathlessly trying to give him a sense of what life was like in college. When I finally stopped talking he nodded in that way of his and kept his eyes on the road.

After an hour or so we hit Calvert County. I craned my neck around to catch all of those familiar signs as they sailed past us in the dark. Adam's Rib, Buehler's Market, Dorsey Auto Sales, even the Walmart. When my father turned left at the four-way light on Ball Road, where our old church glowed like a lantern up on the hill, he pointed out a new sign on the corner. It had been a few years now since the scandal had hit Rock Church, when Bishop Gimenez had admitted to an affair with a younger woman. Once the news came out, Pastor Jim changed the name of the church, and one of the elders borrowed a bulldozer and hauled away the big white rock that had stood for years like a sentinel on that steep hill.

I asked my father if he'd ever been back and he shook his head, saying that it had felt like the Lord had removed his blessing from the congregation. After the scandal, Pastor Jim had become vindictive and angry, and one day my father walked out and never returned. Now he and my mother went to a Baptist church on the northern end of the county.

A few miles east of the church my father turned onto an unmarked, pitted dirt road and slowed to an idle to put the truck into four-wheel drive. The truck tunneled through a half mile of dark woods, and then the trees suddenly opened up into a vast expanse of snow-covered farmland. My father followed the faint divots in the rutted-out driveway, through the fields toward a three-acre swatch of rich bottomland on top of a hill. My family had moved just after I left for college, and my father told me that on the other side of the hill, you could follow a trail for a half mile and get to the cliffs that cut the land off from the mouth of the Chesapeake Bay. It was well past two in the morning when we climbed out of the truck, but my mother was wide-awake, waiting for us on the wide porch of the small white farmhouse. She offered to heat up a plate of roast chicken and I shook my head, collapsing onto the couch and pulling my wet sneakers off. She picked them up and laid them out on some old newspaper in front of the heating duct, so they'd be dry by morning.

※

The next day we all gathered around the kitchen table and held hands while my father said a blessing. In the few months that I'd been gone Obere had bulked up and sprouted a beard, and Sam was nearly the height of my father. Only Joshua seemed the same. He was six years old now, blond and quick to laugh. It took us less than ten minutes to tear through the breakfast my father made—scrambled eggs, fried potatoes, a heaping pile of bacon, and white toast dripping with butter and grape jelly—but we sat around the table for another hour or so, telling stories. Our favorite ones were about my father. We laughed ourselves into near-seizures recounting the time my father broke a wooden spoon on my brother's thigh, the time my father slept in a tent for two weeks before letting his anger drop and speaking to us again, the time he kicked me out of his pickup truck after an early morning argument about the nature of free will, leaving me to make my way to a gas station to call my mother to pick me up.

My father smiled ruefully as he listened to us talk, shaking his head as if reminded of the behavior of a long-forgotten uncle prone to half-baked stunts. He was older now. From my mother's phone calls I knew his rage hadn't completely disappeared, but his body no longer supported it—the words that stung when they came from a black-bearded, suntanned man lost their power when they came out of this man's mouth. My mother was relieved when we ran out of stories and shooed us out of the kitchen so she could start baking.

Late in the afternoon Joshua and I borrowed my father's truck to make one last run to Walmart for last-minute presents. We got a crockpot for my mother and finally decided on a hummingbird feeder for my father and some DVDs for Obere and Sam. On our way back home we passed the live nativity on the hill on the corner of Route 4 and Ball Road, in front of our old church. As we waited for the light to turn green I honked my horn and Joshua rolled down his window and waved. Mary and Joseph and the wise men waved back enthusiastically and one of the angels twirled.

I told Joshua about the time when we were the ones up on that hill. My mother wore a maroon bathrobe and thermal underwear, I had angel wings strapped over my winter coat, and Obere and Sam wore makeshift shepherds' cloaks that my mother had made by cutting holes in army blankets. Joshua was a baby then and he lay in the manger with two sleepers on underneath a puffy yellow coat. A few single men from the church had been cajoled into becoming wise men for a night. My mother had coached them in their wardrobe, recommending purple and red, and brought them paper crowns and some of my costume jewelry. One of them still smoked—the Holy Ghost had not yet released him from his old habits. Two of the men submitted to their crowns and drew the line at the jewelry, but the smoker had pierced his ear long ago and had been delighted to find a gold hoop in the jewelry box. My father had his doubts, but their consensus was that the earring looked Middle Eastern.

I remembered it as if it had happened that morning. When my father set up the generator and plugged the lights in, Obere had slid down the hill and scurried across the street, shouting for us to turn a little to the left. When he ran back up, breathless, he reported that we all gleamed against the darkness, and you couldn't tell my mother was wearing a bathrobe. So we were ready. At first my mother arranged us carefully, encircling the cradle where Joshua had been propped up on pillows. The tight formation lasted about a half an hour, after which Joshua needed to be nursed and things fell apart. My brothers, being shepherds, were allowed to tear around the hill, as long as they didn't get close to the edge. My father got into a civil argument about infant baptism with one of the wise men. I waited expectedly in my angel outfit, watching the cars zip south. The soft light of twilight faded into something deeper. The air was cold enough for snow, but it held off. Approaching cars slowed, sometimes honking, and we would all cheer and smile, even my father. At that time I imagined the cars held people just like us, mothers singing Christmas songs to keep their broods happy. Their problems would be our kind of problems—not enough money for the gas bill, a stolen toy, an unexpected curse from the father. But now I knew better. Not many families had been like us.

From his perch next to me on the bench seat of the truck, Joshua shook me out of my reverie, asking for more stories about the old days. I obliged him, dredging up memories about long-lost pets and various misadventures, and he looked contented. He barely remembered the days when we were all together, under the same roof, sharing a home, a God, and a vocabulary. It seemed like we had lost that now, and there was no path back to the time when threads of belief stitched our family together at the seams.

After dinner my family bundled up in sweaters and scarves to go to the Christmas Eve service at their new Baptist church in Prince Frederick. When my mother asked me to come I shook my head and kept my eyes on my magazine, afraid to look up and see the disappointment in her face. She probably thought I was going to sneak out to meet my cousins at Boyle's Tavern for spiked cider. That was true, but that wasn't the whole story.

I knew how those Christmas Eve services went. First the old hymns with their strangely affecting lyrics, then one of the deacons' wives singing her heart out to some jazzed up Christmas carol, then the children's pageant with all those kids in halos and wings, and then a sermon carefully designed to open up your heart and probe its innermost recesses. And then they'd pass out the candles and the lights would dim, and there would be one last hymn. One of the slow ones that always brought tears to my eyes. I didn't think I could get through the service, even though part of me wanted to join my family in a back pew. I was afraid those old hymns would tug open my doubt like a pulled stitch.

❦ Chapter 9 ❦

Forgiven

When I returned to school I kept having the feeling that I was living on a different planet than the one I was used to, one with a slightly different molecular composition and a stronger gravity. I felt dizzy all the time and couldn't stand up for long periods. That spring I scheduled all of my classes in the afternoons, so I could stay up all night and sleep all morning. The structure of that school was so open that it was easy for me to slip away. I still couldn't afford a meal plan, so I survived on snacks I charged at the school store and bagels my friends snuck out of the cafeteria. I was already so thin and my weight dropped off even more, until I stopped feeling hunger in the same way I used to. I made it almost to Easter before my friends insisted I make an appointment with health services.

The doctor who examined me was a plain-faced woman with glasses and a straight brown bob. She checked my blood pressure and pressed the cold stethoscope against my ribcage, then she asked me to wait in the lobby for a few minutes. For nearly half an hour I read pamphlets about preventing STDs and eyed the fishbowl of multicolored condoms and dental dams near the door. When she called me back into her office she stated the facts clearly and without emotion. She said it was past time for residential treatment. She had already phoned the insurance company to get their authorization, and she thought she might be able to get a spot for me at a center in Philadelphia for women with eating disorders.

I protested. I told her I knew I was too thin, but there was no way I was anorexic. I didn't hate my body. I pointed to the concern of my childhood doctors for proof—how that one doctor had told my mother to deep-fry all my vegetables so I'd gain weight. Then I explained about the meal plan issue—how all first-year students were required to be on the meal plan, but I'd slipped through the cracks because of a last-minute change in my housing assignment, and the mistake had never been caught. She didn't say very much, just asked me questions and scribbled in her legal pad with a ballpoint pen. Finally she interrupted me.

"Jessica, I'm going to stop you for a second," she said, pushing her glasses farther back on her nose. "Right now you weigh ninety-six pounds. You are five feet eleven inches tall. Sit with that for a minute."

I sighed and stretched my hands to my legs, then twirled my hair and shrugged.

"Let me tell you what that says to me," said the doctor. "It says that you are in grave danger. Your body is not getting enough carbohydrates, so it has started consuming muscle. You said that your periods have stopped. That's a huge red flag. It means that your body has begun shutting down."

My face flushed. I tried the trick of finding a still point and locking into it, so that everything else faded away. I used to do it when I was younger and my father started raging when he drove me to school. But the sheer beige panels covering the windows made the room so dim that I couldn't find a place to fix my gaze. I tried the bookshelf, running my watering eyes over all those blurry titles, trying to find one I could stick with. There. *Manson's Tropical Diseases*.

"I want you to get in touch with the feelings that you're having right now," the doctor said gently.

I stayed focused on *Manson's Tropical Diseases* and tried to do as she said, but my mind felt cold and mineral and seamless, like marble or steel. For a minute I broke my gaze away from the book and met her eyes. They were warmer and brighter than I expected, a brassy brown. I saw that she was trying and part of me felt sorry for her.

"I don't feel anything," I said, and gave her a small smile.

᠁

My mother drove up from Maryland to help me pack my things and deliver me to the rehabilitation center. The day we arrived my father drove up to Philadelphia from Maryland with all three of my brothers and we crammed into the therapist's office for my intake interview. The therapist's name was Rebecca and she was a thin, sharp woman, quiet with a serious air. She wore pearls, a dark-knit, loose-fitting collared dress, black-rimmed glasses with delicate frames, and nude lipstick. She pursed her lips and nodded in greeting and we all sat gingerly on the sofas. Joshua had trouble keeping his hands to himself.

Rebecca kept saying the word "anorexia" and every time she did my mother flinched. Rebecca explained that the treatment environment the Renfrew Center provided was carefully calibrated to provide both structure and support, so residents could stabilize medically and normalize their eating. She talked about twenty-four-hour nursing care and

psychotherapy groups, of early morning weigh-ins and in-
dividual and family therapy. Art therapy. Body tracings.
Ensure Plus. Nutritionists. Vital signs. Group meetings.
Psychotherapy. The words came so fast we couldn't quite
catch the line of what she was saying, but none of us stopped
her. My stomach jumped around in my belly like some kind
of panicked animal. I decided in that moment that I would
think of myself as a reporter. I had been taking a journalism
class, and burying myself in the healthy distance of a writer
sounded like a tremendous relief. I'd take notes about this
place and its strange ways. That idea gave me the courage I
needed to tune into Rebecca again.

"You'll be part of Jessica's journey too," she was telling
my parents. "You're fairly close, in Maryland? If you can
come up on Friday afternoons for our family weekends, we
can schedule our family therapy sessions then. We tend to
see the greatest strides when families are an integral part of
the treatment team."

A sob cut across the room. My mother was weeping.
Mascara-stained tears dripped down her face, cutting lines
across her foundation. My father clenched his jaw and I
looked at Rebecca with misery. My mother wrung her hands
and for a minute it looked like she was going to get a hold
of herself, then she broke down again. Through her tears
she said, "This is so new to us. We're a happy family. I don't
know what we did wrong, for things to be like this."

At that moment Joshua grabbed at one of tchotchkes on
the bookshelf, and it dropped to the wood-paneled floor
with a clatter. Rebecca winced and gave my mother a tight
smile, then she offered her some tissues.

Each morning the night nurse woke me up at quarter to five for the morning weigh-in. I padded after her in my slippers to the office, then drank the meal-replacement shake required if my weight didn't match the target gain for the day. At breakfast I picked up my tray and ate quickly, then grabbed my coat and had a cigarette before the support groups and therapy sessions started up. Our days were planned in fifteen-minute increments, chiseled into schedules. I didn't resist any of the rules or regulations, even the minor ones about where you could or couldn't smoke. None of us did. We were like sheep, glad for the shepherd.

I studied the other women as we sat three to a table in the dining hall. The bulimic women, Ava and Maggie, still had a little color in their cheeks, but the anorexic women, like Claire and Sadie, looked like ghosts. They had a certain pallor about them that makeup couldn't hide, and tended to drown their skeletal frames in long sleeves and pants a size too big. Counselors circulated through the dining hall to keep an eye on us while we ate, checking the trays before we threw them away and writing down everything that was left uneaten. Despite the close observation, Claire still toyed with her food, tearing pieces of bread into little bits and lining up peas and bits of carrot in a row before piercing them one by one with a single tine of her fork. That kind of thing wasn't really allowed, but the counselors left her alone as long as she ate everything eventually.

In the haze of my new routine I cultivated a demented brand of cheerfulness. Every afternoon I dutifully filled out the menu worksheets for the next day, adding up my calories. I was supposed to have over three thousand a day, so I chose the highest calorie content—two chocolate milks, a piece of cherry pie, six packets of half-and-half in my coffee. After all, the jig was up. There was no use resisting the program and risking lengthening my stay. Privately I felt that I was an easier case than the other women. They were clearly troubled, whereas I was just going through a bad patch. But after a few days at Renfrew I began alternating between that position and the position that things were worse than I had thought.

⟨⟩

The following week, Rebecca and I met again in her small office in the heart of the manor house. As she gathered her papers together I looked around the room and saw that it was decorated with small abstract paintings in brown and orange, each carefully framed. I guessed they were probably from former patients. I didn't dare comment on them for fear that she'd think I was reading something into them.

"I was reflecting on our conversation a few days ago, and I have some questions for you," she said, pulling out her legal pad and flipping through the pages. She probed at the story I'd told her—our poverty, my father's anger, the drugs I'd tried in high school and college, my bisexuality, my father's discovery of my journal. I'd grown used to telling my story through the years and I unpacked it for her. No, we weren't abused. My father spanked us and sometimes used a belt or a switch on my brothers, but that was what people did. Yes, we were poor, but we always had enough to eat. Yes, I missed my family. After a while Rebecca said it sounded as if I had overcome a lot to make it to college, and I must have felt good about that. I realized I was shaking my head.

"What part of that statement do you disagree with?"

I stared at my lap, trying to ignore the burning sensation in my sinuses. I wasn't going to let myself cry. Rebecca looked at me with a pinched expression.

"You look angry," she said.

I shook my head again. Actually I was furious. But I wasn't going to give her the pleasure of knowing that. There was no point in correcting her misconceptions. She lived in a world orthogonal to mine. She had pearls in her ears and an expensive haircut. Her parents probably owned some hundred-year-old stone house in Connecticut and vacationed in Martha's Vineyard for two weeks every summer. She grew up in the same world she lived in now, listening to rock music and believing in evolution without ever feeling guilty about it. She'd never had to make a choice between the past and the future.

"What are you thinking about?"

My eyes rested on an ugly little mud-colored painting in a gold-edged frame, and I found myself telling Rebecca about a time that I was looking through the old steamer trunk at the end of my mother's bed and found a piece of loose-leaf paper. She'd written out a list of what her life was like before and after she'd met the Lord. One side chronicled all her insecurities: her stuttering, her anxiety, and the loneliness she'd felt growing up in her mother's house once her parents separated and her sisters left home. On the other side were the names of her children, her status as a wife and mother, and the many ways she ministered to others through the church. Even her handwriting changed when she listed her blessings, becoming fuller and more confident.

I told Rebecca that I understood how my mother, having found the key to fulfillment in her life, would want to give that experience to everyone she met. She was a shy woman, not comfortable talking to strangers, but whenever she saw someone begging for food or looking upset, she'd make her way over to them and offer a hand, speak to them quietly, slip them a few dollars for some food. And then she'd start talking to them about Jesus and what he had done for her, and what he could do for them. She'd pull out a slip of paper and write down the number of a food pantry. Maybe she'd make plans to pick them up for church. She wanted strangers to know God's love, so how much more did she want that for me? But instead of getting the daughter she deserved, who would be happy and satisfied with life in the county and marriage to a God-fearing man, she got a daughter who rolled her eyes when she was the unwilling recipient of lengthy prayers. But that didn't stop my mother from trying to bridge the gap. She loved me and wanted me to have access to the faith that had given her so much comfort. Above all she wanted us to be together in eternity.

Before I walked away from the church, my family and I used to look in the same direction, toward the same sun. We believed there was one God and he was looking on us with love, because we were his children and we followed his commandments. There were those on the margins—my aunt who smoked cigarettes, Catholics, or the people who went to the mosque across the street from the hospital. But no one in our community would actually deny the existence of God.

That day in the bathroom when I wrote my name on that piece of paper, I slipped outside the circle, and outside the circle was death. There was no future, no past. Maybe that was why I couldn't gather up the energy to focus on my classes, to follow the rules I charted out for myself. I was already outside of the only world that mattered, and I didn't know what to move toward. So instead I drifted, chasing sensation, making do with what I had. As I sat there in Rebecca's office, I realized I didn't know how to live differently. I had friends, but I wanted a family. I had passions, but I wanted something to believe in.

※

A few days later I stood in line for my midday dose of clonazepam—for anxiety—and paroxetine—for depression—and then shuffled to the eastern side of the manor house for the residents' support group. Jill, the social work intern, facilitated the session. She had fat ringlets of blond hair with dark roots and a singsong voice she used to thank us for any minor contributions to the discussion.

I settled myself in my chair and looked over at the women in the circle next to me: Sweet Sadie, who lived in a mini-mansion in Georgetown with her high-profile politico parents. Ava, whose little sisters ran to her room to embrace her every time they came to visit. Maggie from Appalachia, so embarrassed of her thick accent that she hardly spoke. Claire, one of the walking ghosts, fresh out of the hospital where she had had a feeding tube put in.

Over the past few weeks I'd heard most of the other women's stories. They all sounded the same. They had high standards for themselves and they never managed to meet them. When things went wrong, they had a habit of turning their pain and frustration around on themselves, so that to the rest of the world they still appeared whole and content, even though on the inside they were slowly dismantling themselves. Each woman was here because there was someone in her life who had blown the whistle and informed the doctors. Things had escalated to a certain point and there was no going back to normal life. But to a woman, no one in my group seemed at all alarmed by how bad things had gotten. They spoke about the series of events that led them to Renfrew with a note of wonder in their voice, as if narrating the plot of a soap opera they'd seen on television.

I knew one of the reasons these women didn't eat was because they weren't that invested in themselves or their survival. Deep down, they didn't think they were worth that much. But looking at them there that day it occurred to me that I had no judgment at all for them, even though I had so much for myself. They were doing the best they could to keep body and soul together. They were wrestling with a sadness that had grown so big and all-encompassing that it had swallowed them up.

I tried to open my mouth. I had a sudden desire to tell them my story, to lay it all out on the table and let them tell me what was what. Was I wrong to walk away from the church? Was it wrong for me to fall in love with a woman? Was I wrong to leave my family and move to Massachusetts for college? I didn't care if Jill the intern listened. I wanted to hear what the other women would say, what they'd think of me. I didn't trust my therapist, but I trusted these women. If they let me off the hook for everything I'd done, then maybe they were right. But when I tried to speak I couldn't stop crying.

Jill blushed. She was used to a few tears, not a fit of hysteria. She stuttered and tried to decide what to do, and that was when Claire got up out of her chair and stooped over me, pressing my wet cheek against her dry, sweet-smelling one and giving me a long, gentle hug. Then Sadie got up. And Ava. They took turns holding me and telling me that it was going to be okay. Jill started to rise but didn't get up. Instead she narrated what was going on, saying, "That's nice, now Sadie is hugging Jessica. She's saying it's okay."

Then Ava's voice cut through Jill's ramblings. I had always thought of Ava as kind of a lightweight, a sorority girl, but with great confidence she disregarded the tacit agreement among the residents that we'd speak as little as possible during group therapy. Instead Ava started talking about how she came home for spring break and eavesdropped on her little sisters as they played dress-up. The girls primped in front of the mirror, sucking in their tiny bellies and mimicking Ava's voice—or maybe their mother's—saying, "I look like a whale! I need to go for a run!" Ava said that their high, girlish voices had haunted her over the next few days, and she started watching those girls closer as they refused dessert and filled up on salad.

A few days later Ava said she went to her mother and father as they sat around the dining room table, knocking back with some wine after dinner, and she told them she was sick and they needed to find her a place where she could get better. She couldn't do it on her own. And then she ended up here. It took everything she had to drink those chalky shakes in the morning and watch the fat creep back onto her waist. But she knew that if she didn't get better—for herself and for her sisters—she wouldn't be able to forgive herself.

"It's been nineteen days," she said, and smiled that same languid smile I used to see on people when they'd just come back from the altar.

There was a buzz of validation. *Thank you, Ava.* Our faces were flushed; we were in a state of deep attention. Ava looked up at me and raised her chin. Something had settled in her eyes. It was my turn now. I nodded and sat up straighter, then I started telling my story. I began with my family: My mother, who loved us fiercely in her gentle way. My father, deeply wounded from his own difficult childhood, whose spiraling rage sometimes got the best of him. My free-wheeling brothers. And then me. Scrawny and shy, the teacher's pet. Endlessly curious, eager to learn and explore. I told them about Pastor Jim and his sermons, and I told them about the church we had built. I told them about Sophie and how flattered I'd been by her attention, how I'd climbed into her embrace and how surprised I'd been when it felt like coming home. I told them how hard I worked to get into college, how the guidance counselor had managed to get waivers for the college admission fees and how I'd nagged my parents to catch up on their taxes so I could apply for financial aid. How I'd holed up in my bedroom studying for the SAT and trying to make sense of the financial aid offers. How excited I was when I found out about the scholarship I'd won, and how my heart had broken open when my father told me my mother still thought I'd come back home one day. But I already knew that I wasn't going back home. I was headed somewhere else, somewhere far from my family and my hometown, far from my childhood faith. But I didn't know where it was, and I didn't know how to get there. And I couldn't forgive myself for leaving in the first place, for walking away when I was so deeply loved.

The air in the room buzzed with energy. It didn't feel like a conference room in a residential treatment center—despite the linoleum and the grey walls and the fluorescent lighting, despite the self-esteem posters taped to the wall. It felt like one of those holy places that people climb mountains or cross deserts to get to, just so they could return to their lives entirely different. The kind of place that could heal the broken parts of you, if you could just suck up the courage to ask for help. When I finished talking I looked around at those women's faces, calm and smiling, stronger than anything I'd ever seen. Their gaze on mine felt like a benediction. A blessing. In the long moments before Jill broke up the circle and ran through her list of announcements, those women's eyes rested on mine, and I felt forgiven.

PART II

❦ *Chapter 10* ❦

Left Behind

I turned twenty-three and twenty-four and twenty-five at the same water-stained mahogany table in the same brick townhouse in Washington, DC, blowing out my candles with the same faces beaming up at me—my roommates and my family, who had driven the hour or so from Maryland. Every morning I woke up in that townhouse, pulled on the same slim-fitting pencil skirts and low heels, and rode my bike south on Mount Pleasant Road and west on Columbia to Eighteenth Street, past bodegas and falafel shops until I reached a gleaming steel-and-glass high-rise on the corner of Connecticut Avenue. I was employed by an aging minister who had founded an interfaith coalition to eliminate nuclear weapons, and I spent my days tucked into a fifth-floor cubicle, crafting catchy headlines for email action alerts and ghostwriting op-eds for bishops and rabbis whose names had more heft than my own. In the evenings I'd strip off those scratchy, synthetic fabrics and curl up in the loft bed of my tiny second-floor bedroom with one of the second-hand paperbacks I'd dragged around with me since I first left home. But I never finished them. Instead my roommate

Annie would knock on the door and we'd squeeze ourselves into tank tops and mini-skirts in reds and electric blues and go dancing at Chief Ike's Mambo Room, or Jared would text me to come meet him at the Raven, a smoky, dimly lit dive bar in the middle of Mount Pleasant.

I felt useful for the first time in my life, but after a few years everyone I knew seemed to be leaving. Annie went off to London to study sustainable energy, and then she found a job working for a solar advocacy group. Jared left to travel in Europe for six months, and another friend fell in love with a farmer's son in central Maine and moved there to start a homestead. They had each developed some great passion, for a person or a place or a cause. I wanted that for myself, and every so often I caught the tail of that feeling, but it was a slippery thing that seemed to go out of my grasp as soon as I had made contact with it. Instead I ricocheted from love to love, picking up temporary passions and then putting them aside again.

And then a whirlwind came my way. After years of dating mostly women, I fell in love with a man, a bearded lawyer from Texas with a messy mop of brown hair and grease stains on his jeans from the stripped-down road bike that he rode all around the city. He had shoulders like a rugby player and West Texas manners. When we met at a bar in Columbia Heights, he gripped my hand so hard I had to shake it out afterwards. "You have a really strong handshake," I told him. "You're really pretty," he responded.

Alex marched through life purposefully, firmly grounded in the physical world. He was always moving, never settled, but something about his manic energy made me feel at home. We met in the fall, and by the time the cherry trees around the tidal basin blossomed he had swept me out of my life in

Washington to an adobe cottage nestled in the mountains of Taos, New Mexico, where he had taken a job as an attorney. When I think back to that time it was so stuffed with life that it seemed to glow. In that house I learned to make chicken tortilla soup and carne adovada and fresh tortillas. Alex joined a softball league and I cheered him on from the bleachers with the other players' wives. We adopted a butter-colored cat who sat on Alex's chest while he did sit-ups and then spent the evenings stalking mourning doves in the ravine. We wore out the wildness of our twenties hiking alongside Rio Grande Gorge, splurging on margaritas under the gold-plated ceiling at El Monte Sagrado, skinny-dipping at the hot springs off the mesa, drinking homebrewed beer over an all-night *matanza* in our friend's backyard, playing shuffleboard and buying cigarettes for a quarter apiece at the Alley Cantina, drinking cheap Mexican beer late into the night. The more we drank, the sweeter we were to each other. We drank all the time.

In the spring the cottonwoods rained seedpods down onto the soggy ground and a southern wind blew up from the mountains, bringing the smell of snowmelt with it. In the summer the leaves were green and the air was cool at night, and in the fall the leaves rustled orange and gold and tourists from miles away to see them. In the winter the snow fell from the denim-colored sky in drifts on the street, soft and pillow-like. On Christmas Eve we drove to Taos Pueblo and listened to the priest celebrate mass in the San Geronimo Chapel, then walked outside to sit by the bonfires and watch the procession of the Virgin Mary. On the Fourth of July we drove to Arroyo Seco, where the children painted their faces red, white, and blue and waved American flags to the amusement of their hippie parents. When our friends began having children we lay in our king-size bed and tried to talk ourselves into starting a family.

With every month that passed Alex fell more and more in love with that town. He took up soccer and joined the planning and zoning commission. But over time I grew more and more restless. The life we led seemed at right angles to everything I had known before. As much fun as we had, our lives seemed empty. As the months passed, a drumbeat started up again inside me, a strange and nervous energy that made it feel impossible to continue the old routine of meeting Alex's colleagues for drinks on Friday night, watching his softball games on Saturday mornings, and going grocery shopping on Saturday afternoons.

※

After a year in the mountains we moved to a small adobe cottage on a street lined with cottonwoods, just next to the town plaza. At the corner was a small Spanish-style church, a low-to-the-ground adobe building with a dark-brown cross nailed to the roof. It was an Assembly of God church, run by a pastor with the same story all the Pentecostal pastors had—lost and then found. Twice on Sundays and once on Wednesday nights the parking lot filled with chattering families. I saw myself among the girls—their dark ponytails bobbing behind them as they raced around the parking lot in patent leather shoes, floral dresses, and thick coats. They disappeared into the church for a few hours and I could hear the high hum of the worship service through the thick adobe walls. When they spilled into the parking lot again, wrapped up in their winter things, there was a new liveliness in their eyes.

On Sunday afternoons I watched them from the living room window as I drank tea curled up on the couch. One day, Alex ambled in from the bedroom, pulling his thermal running jersey over his head as he prepared to go out for a run, and made a snarky comment about the families who wasted a gorgeous Sunday morning cooped up in that church. I felt a rush of anger toward Alex and found myself snapping at him, telling him to shut up. What did he know about the transcendent? He lived in a world of things. There was a whole dimension of life that he'd never know or understand—the strange pleasure of keeping your body and mind pure, the raw terror of the coming apocalypse, that washed-clean feeling you had when you walked out of the church on Sunday. Alex's world was one of action and sensation, and try as I might, I couldn't get comfortable in it.

A wedge started growing between us. I'd always had a bit of my father's temper, and it started flaring up at odd moments. I'd be washing carrots idly, chopping garlic, and then my blood would start simmering. I'd clench my lips closed and concentrate on the chopping, until Alex would ask me for a spatula or something, and then all holds were off. I can still see his face, surprised at first, like a toddler walking blithely through the park, thinking he's holding his father's hand before looking up to see a stranger. Then his own blood charged him up with adrenaline and fury, and we would fight over the food we were cooking. Later in bed we'd edge away from each other, cocooning ourselves far into the separate corners of our king-size bed until it felt like we were sleeping alone. Eventually I applied to graduate school and got into a three-year program at the University of Houston. Alex promised to take the Texas bar exam, but none of our friends were surprised when a few months later I ended up moving to Texas by myself.

※

Seven years after the collapse of Enron, Houston was a sprawling city that seemed to multiply on a daily basis, without the limitations of zoning. The downtown was packed with men in thousand-dollar suits and skyscrapers housing multinational oil and gas corporations, and my neighborhood in Montrose was full of bars and tattoo shops and townhouses under construction. I rented a four-hundred-square-foot garage apartment with a tilting floor and paid a guy on Craigslist a hundred dollars to go around with me in his pickup truck, loading up on cheap furniture from thrift stores.

My graduate program demanded a great quantity of reading and teaching, and I was dutiful, spending long stints at bookstores and coffee shops, reading Shakespeare and Woolf and Plato, grading my composition students' triple-spaced summary-and-analysis papers. During the week my teaching schedule and coursework kept me upright, showered and dressed at regular intervals, but on the weekends I felt alone and untethered. In spare moments I tried to write fiction, but doing so required a certain kind of faith—in the words of William Maxwell, to send a hunting dog out and trust that he'll come back with a bird in his mouth. But I was filled with doubt and my stories all had a short leash. The main character was always a stunted version of me.

I started spending Saturdays and Sundays on my couch in my pajamas, unwashed and nervous, watching movies on my laptop and reading novels, leaving the house only for takeout or to meet friends at a bar once night fell. When I did go out the conversation dragged, always circling around to the same things, but when I stayed home my apartment felt small and tight. It started sinking in that I had traded one cage for another. I tried to untangle the threads of what had gone wrong, but it was like trying to fold a king-size sheet in a space no bigger than a shoebox. I couldn't unpack it all. I couldn't make it neat. How had I ended up, at nearly thirty years old, broke and alone in the middle of a web of asphalt and highways, in a decrepit apartment with rotten beams and a crooked door? I couldn't understand it, but I knew it had something to do with the deep dissatisfaction I had with the flat contours of ordinary life, a voice inside me that kept asking, *Is this all there is?*

❦

At a house party later that fall I met a poet named Max with a long white beard. When we found out that we had both grown up Pentecostal, we retreated to the rickety back porch with our beers and split a pack of American Spirits. We told each other stories about the days when we thought we'd be carried out of the calendar at any minute, to a realm outside of time and language. Max went first. He leaned back against the wet, splintered wood and told me about something that happened to him when he was eight years old. The school bus dropped him off in front of his suburban home outside of Houston. He opened the door, threw off his backpack, and began calling out to his mother and brother and sister, but the house was quiet and still. His mother's purse was in its usual spot on the dining room table, the cereal bowls still filled the sink, and his brother's and sister's toys littered the floor. He walked to the front of the house and saw that his mother's station wagon was still in the driveway, and that's when his heart started hammering.

Max raced through the bedrooms, opening closets and looking under beds, hollering names into the basement and laundry room, and then with a sickening realization he knew exactly what had happened. The trumpet had blown but he hadn't heard it. His family had floated up to heaven to meet the Lord in the sky, and he had been left behind to face the end of the world alone. By the time his mother came home from a neighbor's house with his brother and sister in tow, he was rocking on the floor, inconsolable, tears running down his face and snot plugging up his nose. Max was probably in his forties when he told me the story, but the beer in his right hand still shook a little when he talked about it.

I smiled and started telling my own stories. The way we'd celebrate Hallelujah Eve instead of Halloween at our church, building a bonfire and throwing ungodly books and records in. The time my brother's cheeks broke out into a rash, which continued until we watched the 700 Club and heard a word from the Lord that there was a child out there afflicted with red cheeks because of too much citrus. My mother cut the oranges out of his diet and the rash stopped immediately.

Max grinned so I kept going. My father's naming his firstborn son Obere—a word he'd never heard before—because he thought he'd heard the name directly from the Lord in a dream. The time I had approached my father after getting stuck on a strange passage from Genesis in which Onan "spilled his seed on the ground" rather than obey the biblical commandment to impregnate his brother's widow and bring her children into his household. I couldn't understand why God would put Onan to death for knocking over some vegetable seeds and asked my father to explain it. His mouth turned up into a strange kind of smile and he said he didn't understand it either. "Let's pray about it," he said. "We'll pray God will reveal himself to us in that passage." But he warned me that not all would be revealed immediately.

I saved the best story for last. A visiting evangelist stopped me after church when I was twelve. He was a dashing African American man in a three-piece suit and snakeskin shoes, from one of the Carolinas. He'd given a sermon about asking and receiving, and it had been a hit. Everyone came to the altar to put their troubles down and walk away lighter. A half hour after the service wrapped up, I was moping around the foyer waiting for my parents to finish whatever conversations were keeping them. That's when the minister walked through the swinging doors to the sanctuary with some of the elders and bounded over to me in just a stride or two. He sized me up from several feet above me. I was all knees in my too-short Sunday dress and patent leather Mary Janes.

Then he bent down level with me and up close he smelled like mint and cologne. "Hallelujah," he said quietly, and put his arms on my shoulders while the elders smiled behind him in a proprietary way. In a booming voice he told me he had a prophecy for me. He said that God had ordained that I would be a writer, and I would write my first book by the time I was sixteen. He even had a vision of what it would look like: a slim, ivory-colored volume with a portrait of Jesus on the cover. I was thrilled, but not at all surprised. I was used to living in a magical world, so it didn't surprise me that God had whispered in this fragrant man's ear and sent him in my direction. We didn't know each other, but we had a Spirit in common, and with just one look he could tell the desires of my heart. He could see me flopped on top of my white ruffled canopy bed, spending hours scribbling stories about rabbits and girls with glasses who looked and thought like me.

Max laughed again, softer than before. "You ever write that book?" he asked me.

I shook my head and took a long drag of my cigarette. When I was a kid I had tortured myself with that prophecy, convinced it would have come true if I hadn't been so lazy, so incapable of sitting down and writing the book that God wanted me to write. Maybe it was no coincidence that I had walked away from the church before I turned sixteen.

Max and I smoked companionably, savoring the quiet and the chilly air and the thick, decadent scent of the jasmine that wafted up from the hedgerows in the back alley. It was a lovely night, one of those chilly evenings in early April that were all the more precious because we knew that soon the heat would crank up like a furnace and we'd be stuck in our air-conditioned apartments. After a few minutes the porch filled up with other smokers and then the moment was gone. I stayed on the stairs arguing with someone about the symbolism of the turtle in that Edward Hoagland essay and Max went back in to dance. But at the end of the night when only the drunks were left, he caught my eye across the crowded room and nodded, a sad half-smile on his face.

I knew what he was thinking. He and I used to live with the feeling that at any moment the world would erupt and the daily would be blown open at last. The Lord would come back to take his rightful place on the throne and the faithful would finally get their just reward. We wouldn't be on the outside anymore, struggling to explain ourselves and our strange ways to the nonbelievers. God's plan would come into stark and perfect fulfillment. But the years went by and nothing happened. The world didn't end. There was no eruption. We kept on waking up to another day in which the sun stayed bright in the sky, another day where we were still stuck in the same bodies, the same stale lives. It took faith to believe that change could still be possible, and we were fickle people who had a hard time loving what we couldn't see. Eventually we gave up and stopped believing in anything at all.

₡

That night I walked the mile and a half home to my garage apartment on West Main Street. It was farther than I'd ever walked by myself before, all the way from Hyde Park past the gay bars on Taft and Fairview. It was late and there were hardly any cars, just a few guys on bikes. Barbacks probably, on their way home after a long night. The air was still clear and clean. I'd slept late that morning and had moseyed around the house all day, reading a little and straightening up, cooking sweet potatoes, grading some papers. All day long I'd felt foggy but now I felt wide awake, exhilarated. It had been a long time since I had talked to someone who had grown up haunted by the same ghosts as I was. Twenty years had passed since I first walked away from the church, but lately I'd been thinking about the girl I used to be. The zealot. Scrawny and shy, seventy-five pounds soaking wet, operating with the only currency she had. She knew she wasn't enough on her own. She needed to make allegiances. She wanted power, the kind that heals the sick and raises the dead and lifts small girls from backwoods farm towns into the glittering, bustling, half-evil world. A world that for all its faults was still beloved to God. Back in my apartment, I lay awake listening to the air conditioner humming and rattling, a tight feeling deep in my gut.

That feeling stayed there for weeks, until one Sunday morning I woke up and went out on the porch. The sky was white instead of blue and a light rain was falling that had a strange smell to it, like some feral animal. I felt empty and leftover, untethered. I walked back into the house and showered with real fervor, scrubbing shampoo into my hair and raking a bar of soap over my arms and legs and belly. I pulled on one of the dresses I usually wore when I taught and drove to a church I'd noticed a few weeks before. It was one of those newfangled emergent churches and the building where the service was held looked like a warehouse. A chattering crowd was packed into the building's foyer, while a team of tattooed baristas took orders at the coffee shop that flanked one of the walls. I slipped through the crowd and made my way to one of the back rows in the sanctuary, nodding to the young families sitting next to me and feeling a little dizzy. When the worship service began I sang haltingly along with the hymns, following the lyrics as they were projected on the white wall above the stage. Before the sermon there was a video about the relief work the church was doing, building wells in Central America, and then the sermon dealt with God's promise to his chosen people. The pastor wore jeans and a goatee and sipped coffee while he preached, and throughout the length of his sermon a woman stood at the side of the stage, painting a picture at an easel. A stone being rolled away. I listened to the sermon warily, ready to walk out in the event of some sly reference to gay marriage or abortion, but the sermon was light and the pastor seemed gentle, tender-hearted. When I walked out of the sanctuary an hour later, ducking out of the coffee hour and striding quickly toward my car, I was filled with relief and exhaustion, as if I had run a mile in the Texas heat. I drove home and slunk into bed, my head throbbing.

✤

For years I'd refrained from talking about my childhood faith, but that spring it seemed to come up constantly. When one of my fellow graduate students, a hipster kid from New Jersey in skinny jeans, made an offhand reference to Holy Rollers in one of my seminar classes, I surprised myself by pushing back angrily, defending the people who I myself had ridiculed for most of my adult life. The other students in the seminar squinted at me as I went on about how it felt to go about your life believing that you were one of God's chosen people. My professor was one of those endlessly curious academic types, and after class he pulled me aside and asked if Pentecostalism was native to the southern United States or if it had actually started elsewhere. As he looked at me expectantly I realized I had no idea. When I was a girl experiencing it for the first time, that rollicking religion seemed to have come organically, from the world itself, like water or air. Pentecostals aren't much for history, and the only origin story I'd ever heard was the story of how the Holy Spirit had descended on Jesus's disciples centuries ago when they gathered to mourn his death.

When I got back to my apartment that night I opened my laptop and started reading about the early days of the church. The groundwork for the birth of Pentecostalism had been laid a century before, when circuit riders tore through the countryside, preaching God's word and pumping people into a frenzy. It was a time of great optimism and great impatience. The optimism came from the feeling that something could still be done to redeem the world before the Lord's return, to save those who still needed to be saved. The impatience came from the feeling that time was short, that any day the promised smoke and fire and vapor would swallow up the faithful and heathen alike.

At a revival in Cane Ridge, Kentucky, twenty thousand people gathered to worship. Seven men preached at once at different spots in the tent, telling their listeners that God used to speak to people directly and personally, that he was capable of healing the sick and raising the dead. They told stories of how the Lord manipulated physical matter for his own purposes and spoke to people in their own languages, if they could just forget themselves long enough to tune into his wavelength. They pleaded with their listeners to give up swearing and gambling and adultery, and to cleanse and purify themselves so God might see fit to touch them. They claimed that if people could just quiet their hearts, they might be able to hear the voice of God, shimmering through the air, struggling to make itself heard.

Their message fell on fertile ground. "The noise was like the roar of Niagara," wrote a participant. "The vast sea of human beings seemed to be agitated as if by a storm." In another account, someone wrote, "The people fell before the Word, like corn before a storm of wind, and many rose from the dust with divine glory shining in their countenances." A Methodist minister told of how he "went through the house shouting and exhorting with all possible ecstasy and energy." He wasn't the only one with a physical response. Some began contorting as they sobbed and shouted. "Their heads would jerk back suddenly, frequently causing them to yelp, or make some other involuntary noise. . . . Sometimes the head would fly every way so quickly that their features could not be recognized. I have seen their heads fly back and forward so quickly that the hair of females would be made to crack like a carriage whip, but not very loud."

The miracle they were waiting for finally happened at midnight on the first day of the new millennium. In a Bible school in Kansas City, a milk-fed farmer's daughter named Agnes Ozman lifted her voice to the heavens and got the promised gift. A halo appeared around her head and for three days she could only speak to her classmates in a language that sounded to them like Chinese. A preacher in his late twenties, Charles Parham, who would later become known as the father of Pentecostalism, spread her story far and wide, saying that the languages the Lord had given the apostles in that upper room so long ago had come to life again. Five years later, a revival broke out in a storefront church in the middle of a ghetto in Los Angeles. Hundreds of worshippers, Black and white together, packed into a tiny wood-frame church on Azusa Street. The church was poor, and the congregation lacked hymnals or programs, and used a stack of wooden crates in place of a pulpit. I could picture them, the men in beards, their hands work-worn and flecked with cuts and scars, their boots tracking in hay and giving off the smell of livestock. The women might have looked delicate in their Sunday dresses, but their hands were rough. They had no patience for high rhetoric or fancy turns of phrase. They knew what was good and they knew what was evil.

Their pastor was William Seymour, the son of former slaves, who had been exiled to the hallway back in Bible college because of his race. He had made the journey to Los Angeles in the segregated car of a train. But none of that mattered now. As he preached, a woman who had never before had a talent for piano played beautiful melodies while singing in Hebrew. People came from all over the country to see it for themselves, so many that the foundation of that little church collapsed, causing the front porch to fall into the yard. Reporters sat in on services and came away with a vague impression of what was going on. One newspaper headline read "Faith Gives Quaint Sect New Languages to Convert Africa." The story continued below the headline in large type: "Votaries of Odd Religion Nightly see 'Miracles' in West Side Room. Led by Negro Elder. The leaders of this strange movement are for the most part Negroes."

Critics from the mainline churches called the new movement "a disgusting amalgamation of African voodoo superstition and Caucasian insanity." Some contacted the police in an attempt to shut the meetings down. They were suspicious of the way races mixed in the new Pentecostal churches and the way God seemed to speak to everyone in the same way, young or old, Black or white, male or female, poor or rich, illiterate or well-read. Frank Bartleman, one of the early scribes of Azusa Street, wrote that it seemed the color line had been washed away in the blood of Jesus Christ.

Reports of healings and miraculous conversions led thousands more to Azusa Street, and soon missionaries sprang out of the church to carry its message around the world. They believed that the strange languages they spoke in—a rollicking, rolling sort of gibberish—were in fact real languages from far-off places. They called them "missionary tongues," and they believed they were a kind of divine shortcut that allowed them to speak directly to the people they wished to convert, without taking the time to learn their languages the old-fashioned way. Charles Parham embraced this view, saying, "Anybody today ought to be able to preach in any language of the world if they had horse sense enough to let God use their tongue and throat."

The zealous poured themselves into the empty places on their maps, so convinced of God's ability to shepherd them that some travelers to Africa or India even refused to take quinine. When pressed, they pointed out that nowhere in the Bible does God endorse pills and powders. When they arrived at their mission sites, many missionaries suffered greatly from malaria, but they received a far crueler blow when they realized they couldn't speak to or understand the people they came to save. Some buckled down immediately to the task of learning languages, while others returned home, their faith shaken.

I read late into the night, following a rabbit trail of hyperlinks, reading about how the religion of my childhood, so marginalized in the United States, was now thriving in every corner of the globe. Scholars described it as the fastest growing religious movement in history. Forty years ago, less than 10 percent of Christians had been Pentecostal, but in another fifteen years, scholars were predicting that one-third would be. And for the first time in history, the majority of them would live south of the equator—in Asia, Central America, and Africa.

I read the story of one Nigerian pastor, Enoch Adeboye, who had grown up in a house made of mud bricks, the first son of his father's third wife. His family were Christians, but whenever sickness or catastrophe struck, they went to the traditional healers for help. Legend had it that when Adeboye was taken to one of these healers as a child, the healer prophesied that he would be a great man, far outshining the other stars in the constellations. Pastor Adeboye had been the first in his family to own a pair of shoes, the youngest instructor in the history of the Nigerian university system, and the first to grow one of Nigeria's small Pentecostal churches into a global megachurch with five million members in Nigeria alone. I'd never heard his name in my life, but the year before *Newsweek* had ranked him alongside Osama bin Laden and President Barack Obama in a list of the world's fifty most influential people. I felt a strange sense of pride in Enoch Adeboye's story, as if he were a cousin or an uncle or some distant relation. He seemed to be the embodiment of my favorite of all of Jesus's promises—that the poor would one day be made rich.

🌿

When I finally glanced at the clock that hung over the couch, it was nearly two in the morning. My phone had long ago gone silent. The bartenders would be shouting about last call and my friends would be closing their tabs and heading home. I yawned and stretched my wrists in small, tight circles, then rubbed my elbows. They'd been pressed against the desk so long that they were imprinted with whorls from the grain of the wood. One more cigarette, I told myself, and then I'd go to bed. I pulled on my peacoat and slipped onto the narrow balcony of my garage apartment, pulling a cigarette from my pocket and lighting it silently. From the shadows below I could hear voices and footsteps, and I pressed against the doorframe to try to make myself invisible to my neighbors as they made their way up the driveway.

The air had gotten colder, but it still felt good. The blood hummed in my veins, fueled by the sudden burst of nicotine, and the pixelated headlines of the articles I'd been reading still swirled in my mind's eye. *Wonderful if true, ignorant girl acquires the gift of tongues.* Nothing was as I expected it to be.

The Pentecostal movement that I had long decried as backwards and closed-minded seemed to be born from a moment of interracial acceptance, and seemed to hold within it the potential for real revolution and change. The God that I had stumbled across through my web search, the God of Agnes Ozman, William Seymour, and Enoch Adeboye, was someone I hadn't thought about in years. I had forgotten about his love for justice and mercy, his preference for the poor. I only remembered his anger and his obsession with purity and control. Eventually I had walked away. But maybe there was a chance I had turned my back on a God who lifted up the poor and downhearted and endowed them with miraculous powers. The God of William Seymour and Enoch Adeboye seemed untouched by conservative politics or moralistic thinking. Their faith seemed clean and good. Maybe it was something I could be proud of after all.

A cat yowled from the roof of a car below, startling me. The night had turned quiet and still. Everyone who had been headed home had likely made it there by now. I ground my cigarette out on the dingy white wooden rail of the balcony, and in the yellow stripe of light that filtered in from the lamp in my living room I noticed a whole row of marks from hundreds of stubbed out cigarettes dappled across the railing. I'd never noticed them before. Now they seemed as ominous to me as the marks a prisoner might scratch into the walls of the cell to track the days.

By the time I pulled off my coat and climbed into bed a few minutes later, I was already gone—back under the revival tent with my hands raised in the air and the language of the Lord in my mouth. A deacon behind me, ready to catch me when I fell. That scene blended in my mind with the scene of that revival in Azusa Street, where so many people crammed together into that tumbledown shack, crying out to God to remove them from the world they knew and lift them up to be with him in heaven. In the morning I'd wake up early and make my way through the maze of live oaks to the university library. I'd bury myself in the story of those early days of the Pentecostal church and follow a winding path through the library stacks to read about how Christianity had upended the global south. I'd sift through the history of the faith I'd walked away from, remembering how it moved me as a child. Maybe somewhere deep inside of me I still wanted to fall, to fall and be caught.

Chapter 11

Made in Nigeria

The more I read, the more I understood: the face of Christianity was changing. Long ago the first Christian missionaries had trickled into the headwaters of the Niger River in twos and threes, clinging to British trade ships and braving malaria to spread the good news to the so-called Dark Continent. But now, just over a century later, private jets left Murtala Muhammed International Airport in Lagos on a daily basis, ferrying Nigerian evangelists toward waiting crowds at churches in Europe, the United States, and elsewhere in the increasingly secular West. Of all the "mushroom churches," as Pentecostal denominations were dubbed by Nigerians, Pastor Enoch Adeboye's church seemed to be growing the fastest. There were six thousand separate congregations in Nigeria and over three hundred in North America. Reporters hadn't been able to verify the church's claim that six million people had once attended a single service in Lagos—but if it was true, that made it the largest Christian gathering in the world.

When I found out that the Redeemed Christian Church of God had spread all the way from Nigeria to Houston, I woke up early one Sunday morning and pulled out various dresses, checking hemlines and necklines until I found something that seemed modest enough to wear to a service. The Pavilion of Redemption rented a thousand-square-foot storefront space in an industrial part of southwestern Houston, about a half hour from my inner-loop apartment. The neighborhood was dotted with gas stations, cash advance depots, and stores advertising prepaid cell phones. As I slowed down on the largely empty highway and searched for the address, I noticed a Korean Pentecostal church and a Spanish-language Pentecostal church occupying the same block. Finally, somewhere off Bissonnet and Southwest Freeway, I spotted the logo of the Redeemed Church—a purple circle with a small white dove at its center.

When I opened the door of the storefront church, the tiny, carpeted room was filled with men and women and children, most in traditional Nigerian dress. Someone had used plastic columns and artificial plants and curtains to set a kind of stage apart from the rest of the room. I tried to hide in the back, but a stern teenage boy in a pin-striped suit escorted me to the very front row. Family after family came over to greet me before the service started, asking my name and what I was up to in Houston. The worship service began with a squeal of music—guitar, a keyboard, and tambourines. If it wasn't for the talking drums—hourglass-shaped drums used for traditional Yorùbá songs—I could have been in the church I grew up in.

The pastor was a slight man in an ill-fitting suit, but his voice was like a thunderbolt. He changed tones easily, moving from gentle to fierce as he prayed over the congregation, and then picked up his gentle tone once again to announce that there would be no sermon today, as it was the first Sunday of the month. Instead, the service would be devoted to testimonies of the ways the Lord worked in our lives. He warned the congregation that this time was meant to be used solely for testimonies, rather than songs. "If you want to sing, then join the choir!" he said sternly.

᠁

For over an hour his parishioners came up to the altar, one after another, young teenagers in fashionable Western clothes and plump grandmothers in dashiki. Everyone started the same way, by praising the Lord, and then launched into stories of how God had touched them. The first person was a delicate-looking teenage girl with wide brown eyes. She announced that by the grace of God she had just graduated from high school. Then came a woman who talked about accidentally leaving her wallet on the hood of the car, going to her job as a prison guard, and then coming back out and finding to her delight that it was still on the hood. "It was God!" she exclaimed loudly, and the whole congregation clapped and whooped.

Multiple people thanked God for not getting a ticket when a police officer pulled them over, two more recent graduates thanked God and their families, and a shy man told of how God came to his rescue when he was trying to turn a rented moving van around in the mountains of West Virginia and got stuck. Another man told the story of finding a wallet and driving to the address listed on the license to return it to a white American woman, who initially refused to open the door to a Black man. "Thank God for not making me a thief!" he said.

Afterwards, while members of the church milled around, squeezing toddlers' cheeks, packing up instruments, and swapping Tupperware containers of hard-to-find Nigerian culinary essentials like yam flour and *gari*, the pastor listened to me prattle on about my research and then flashed a smile, waving away my attempts at an explanation.

"You are welcome here," he said. "All blood runs red in the kingdom of God." And then he invited me to the Redeemed Church's weekend-long Holy Ghost convention the following month, where six thousand Nigerian Christians from all over North America met on a plot of land outside of Dallas for a prayer and miracle service.

It hadn't really made sense for me to go. The convention was in the middle of June, during a heat wave that was epic even for Texas. My ancient Volvo lacked air-conditioning and leaked oil on long road trips, and I could barely afford the gas, much less a hotel room. But for some reason I still dug out my credit card and paid the registration fee.

❦

When the day finally came, I made my way out of Houston with one eye on my oil gauge, whispering a half-ironic prayer that everything would work out. The moon was only a fingernail when I arrived in the tiny town of Floyd, in East Texas, but as I approached Redemption Camp, the flood lights illuminating the parking lot lit up the sky to near daylight. Just past a low-rent trailer park called Mockingbird Estates, a long line of traffic snaked past the sprawling cemetery of a hundred-year-old white clapboard church. As the deeply grooved dirt road doglegged to the right, I braked slowly so as not to spit gravel on the small, hand-lettered sign in front of the church: "Floyd United Methodist, a Church for the Future." And then in smaller type: "Rev. Bill Shaddox." I wondered what the minister thought of his new neighbors. Rev. Shaddox also probably believed that God's hand was alive in the world, but he was probably well aware that if he went to his bishop saying that God had spoken to him and given him a message, the bishop would think the time had come to pack him off to the retirement home.

A whistle blew and a teenage boy in a bright orange vest waved me forward. A hundred yards farther up, dun-colored trailers and modest ranch-style houses gave way to lush cornfields and trees tented with kudzu, and Redemption Camp finally came into view for the first time. I had expected an enormous megachurch, but there wasn't much to see—just a vast expanse of asphalt dotted with stadium lights and an enormous white canvas tent perched on a concrete foundation. The tent looked empty and unoccupied, but as the line of traffic crept closer, the piercing noise of the cicadas gave way to snatches of hymns, the deep-throated trills of a preacher's voice booming from a speaker inside the tent and low murmur of *amen*s coming every minute or so, like a drumbeat. Just past the parking lot, rows of picnic tables were set up and women in traditional Nigerian dress sold *jollof* rice, bean cakes, and peppered chicken at steep prices. Families in African garb—shiny fabrics of orange and red and purple topped off with towering headdresses for the women—and families in Western church clothes crowded around the tables drinking Coke and Fanta from glass bottles.

I followed a crowd of people into the tent and found a seat on a folding chair toward the back, so far from the stage that I had to squint to see beyond the blurs of color. On the projector screen above the stage was a gravelly voiced white woman with thickly applied makeup and a Southern accent. She looked to be in her early fifties. Like so many other

Pentecostal pastors, Sheryl Brady's life was her testimony, and she spent the first portion of her sermon establishing her credentials. She spoke quietly and seriously of pain and torment. She had dropped out of high school at fifteen, cut down by a series of three losses. Her father had died of a heart attack, and her sister had died of hepatitis, and then her mother had been in a terrible car accident. Sheryl married at the age of seventeen, shy and quiet, and had three children before she was twenty. For years she lived from paycheck to paycheck, left out of God's promises, unsure of his plan for her life. Not until her forties did she become a pastor and a conference speaker. Her destiny, she said, had been locked up inside her, and it was only through her faith in God that she was able to draw it out. Now she stood in front of us, an intimidating, perfectly coiffed presence, a lady preacher who shouted like an old-school revival minister.

She read from that chapter from the Book of Luke—the one where Peter, one of Jesus's disciples, went fishing with Jesus. Jesus called him his rock, but Peter was just as much of a doubter as Thomas. Even after seeing miracle after miracle—loaves to fishes, water to wine—he just couldn't open his mind up enough to take in the true nature of the kingdom of God. In this particular story, Peter had been fishing all day and had caught nothing at all. He was back on the shore, cleaning his nets, when Jesus beckoned him out again. He probably hadn't wanted to go, but he listened to Jesus and let down the nets. He caught so many fish that his nets nearly broke.

"Look under your boat," Pastor Sheryl exhorted the congregation. "If you look under your boat, you will see the hand of God holding all those fish back. Jesus was there that day to teach Peter that being a professional fisherman meant absolutely nothing. God is in charge. It doesn't matter how much you study, how much you prepare. Doors will not open for you unless God ordains it. You won't catch a single fish unless God wills it."

Toward the end of her sermon Pastor Sheryl ran her eyes over those many thousands of people and got quiet. Too quiet. She asked us if we were tired, worn out by work and family responsibilities. She looked at us hard and dared us to say it wasn't true.

"Well," she said, "what do you have to show for all that work? Do you have any power? Do you have the ability to heal? Can you lay hands on your body and cast the sickness out? You are closer than you think you are. You have these gifts. Just look under your boat. What does the Bible tell us? Not by might, nor by power, but by the Holy Spirit. You are closer than you think you are to that power," she said, and a hush went through the congregation. "That's why I came to Floyd, Texas," she said in a voice as low and throaty as a lifelong smoker's. "To tell you that you are closer to that power than you think you are."

❦

In a strange coincidence that my mother would have immediately labeled a sign, the first person I met when I pulled up at Redemption Camp again the following morning was the brother of James Fadele, the pastor who had helped establish the United States branch of the Redeemed Church. Pastor Fadele had been charged by Pastor Adeboye with turning what had been a few years ago a sorghum and wheat field into the denomination's North American headquarters. Thanks to his brother's introduction, within twenty-four hours I found myself sitting in Pastor Fadele's palatial home as the stout pastor explained how he found himself in the position of bringing God's word to the heart of East Texas.

"It doesn't come all at once," James Fadele told me, hopping back and forth between tending to his daughters and helping a visiting pastor from Delaware set up a website for his church. He was trying to explain how God's blessing worked. "If it did, God knows we'd run from it. God dips you in, little by little, to see what you can stand."

Pastor Fadele had grown up in the same family compound outside of Lagos where Pastor Adeboye had grown up, but unlike Adeboye, his family was Catholic. "Well, not exactly," Pastor Fadele said, correcting himself. His father had attended Catholic services, but he refused to officially convert to Catholicism because it would have meant abandoning two of his three wives. As a child, Pastor Fadele was a good student and a devout Christian, winning a scholarship to an American university. After graduating he took a job as an engineer and then racked up a number of advanced degrees while he tried his hand at various businesses: first detailing cars, then running a Wendy's franchise.

Once, on a visit to the US, Pastor Adeboye encouraged his friend to start a church, and after initially making some excuses, Pastor Fadele started a small congregation in the basement of his Detroit home. Around that same time, Adeboye had received word from the Lord that Texas was destined to be the North American headquarters of the Redeemed Church. The prophecy was confirmed when a white farmer approached a small group of Redeemed pastors as they sat in a restaurant in Dallas. The man told them that years before, God had instructed him to purchase a hundred acres of pastureland in Floyd. God told him that the land didn't belong to him, but rather a group of "church people."

And then the farmer offered to sell it to the pastors for the same low price he had originally purchased it for.

Soon after he had purchased the land, Adeboye appointed Pastor Fadele as the head of the Redeemed Church's North American division, and Pastor Fadele approached his new mission in the same way he had tackled his business ventures. Within a year, construction had started on the plot of land that would slowly become the mirror image of that eighteen-thousand-acre plot of land in Nigeria, just north of Lagos, where a million worshippers gathered every year for the church's annual convention.

Pastor Fadele told me he had been the one who urged his boss to invest in technology, including a state-of-the-art website that live-streamed Pastor Adeboye's sermons during their Holy Ghost Services in both Lagos and Texas. It was on that website, back in Houston, that I had first been seduced by the church's mission and vision: "to make heaven" and "to take as many people with us as possible." They pledged to plant churches within five minutes' walking distance of every city and town in developing countries, and a five-minute driving distance of cities and towns in developed countries.

"You Americans don't talk about that," he said, removing his delicate glasses to run a handkerchief over them. "You talk about pearly gates and eternal rewards. But Africans believe that we can build a piece of heaven on earth, in our daily lives. Teachers can build heaven at school. Parents can build heaven for their children. And churches can make their congregations a place where God lives and breathes. In Africa, we believe that we can call heaven down to meet us. God wants us to be whole. He wants us to prosper. We don't have to wait until we die to live in glory. We can do that here on earth."

I asked Pastor Fadele about his reception from the white community in Floyd. I myself was dubious. Not that long ago, the road connecting Floyd to the county seat had a banner over it that boasted "Blackest Land, Whitest People." Floyd was settled by hardy pioneers from the Deep South, lured west by the rich Texas Blackland Prairie. They'd brought their conservative brand of Christianity with them, as well as their slaves. Many of the Black residents of Floyd could trace their lineage back to the days when cotton was king and slave labor was the cheapest way to get that cotton out of the ground. Like most other towns in this part of the world, the history of Hunt County was rife with lynchings and other hate crimes. Just six years before the Methodist church up the street was founded, a mob of two thousand white residents overpowered a group of officers and seized a young Black man who had been accused of assaulting a white woman. The next morning they burned him alive in the south side of the town square. Years later, the white residents of Floyd seemed to have nothing but suspicion for their Nigerian neighbors.

"I don't like to be called a racist, but I don't like to be overrun, either," Luanne Moody told a reporter from the *Dallas Morning News* who knocked on the door of her mobile home in Floyd seeking her opinion of the church. "I don't have any problem with black people. . . . I just feel uncomfortable in large numbers of them."

"I'm not a racist," echoed her neighbor, Tina Causey, a sixty-nine-year-old house cleaner, when a reporter from the *New York Times* came calling. "I just don't like a majority of anybody."

"We'll give them some time," Pastor Fadele laughed, smiling so wide that his dimples showed. "Right now they're peeping out the windows, asking each other, where did all those Africans come from? Where did they get those clothes? But then they'll hear the music, they'll feel the Spirit, and they'll come. And we can't wait to have them."

Pastor Fadele rummaged through his briefcase and found the program for the convention, and flipped it open to the governor's letter welcoming the church members to the convention, thanking them for their service, and wishing them success as they worked to lay a strong spiritual foundation for the community. The Hunt County judge wrote a letter as well, offering his prayers that the conference be both divine and sanctified, and asking the Lord to shower the group with peace and holy tranquility. Maybe Pastor Fadele was right. There weren't many other white people at the convention, but the church hadn't been here long. I'd read an article about a church in London, founded by a Nigerian pastor, who regularly hosted four thousand people for its Sunday services.

When I was done asking my questions, Pastor Fadele wanted to know why I'd come to Redemption Camp and why I was so interested in the way they worshipped in Nigeria. I stuttered out an answer, telling him that I had grown up in the church but had gone away from it, and now I was curious about the faith again.

He shook his head knowingly. "God is stirring your heart," he said, and asked me if I'd ever considered traveling to Nigeria. "You won't know what God is doing in my country unless you stand with a million Nigerians at the Holy Ghost Service," he said. "I have a feeling that if you will go there, you will come back changed."

I'm sure my neck flushed, the way it always does when I'm overcome with some strong rush of emotion. I hadn't thought of going to Nigeria until Pastor Fadele said those words, but as soon as that idea was out there in the world it became my idea, and the path immediately unfurled in front of me. I'd find the money. I'd go to Nigeria and immerse myself in the faith I had left as a child.

Months later, when I lobbied my graduate school advisor to change my thesis to an exploration of Nigerian Pentecostalism, I'd make the case that there was a story here, a story that I—being a former believer myself—was highly qualified to tell. I'd position myself as a researcher, an intellectual, not a spiritual seeker making a religious pilgrimage. But even then I sensed that there was something else going on, something that had to do with that wonder-working power that I had sung about as a child. That inchoate thing that surged through the congregation when the worship service had reached its peak, that sudden fierceness in my mother's voice when she prayed over a fever, binding it up and sending the spirit of sickness straight back to the Devil. That strange, upside-down sort of power that I had so craved as a girl. The power that stemmed from obedience and transcended race and class and status. I felt that old longing swell up inside me—a longing to join up, a longing to submerge myself into the body of Christ and forget myself and my own desires.

❦

At nine o'clock on the final night of the revival, praise choirs from congregations all over the country poured in from all sides of the tent. Pastor Fadele took the stage and introduced his mentor to the gathered crowds. "Here is Brother Enoch Adeboye," he shouted, "Made in heaven, born in Nigeria,

exported to the world!" At the sight of the General Over-
seer of the church, the man they affectionately called Daddy
G.O., the tent erupted into an ocean of sound. Pastor Adeboye was a tall man with a broad forehead and a ready smile,
and he wore a bright blue pin-striped suit with a dark-colored
bow tie. As he preached the music slowly swelled up behind
him, keeping step with his throaty, British-inflected voice
as he called heaven down to meet us. Again and again he
talked of power—the electric pulse that lived in each of us,
divinely implanted there by God, doomed to go unused unless we activated it. He promised that if we took full advantage of that power, every evil thing in our life would be
neutralized and we would come into the full manifestation
of what we were intended by God to become.

Every few minutes Pastor Adeboye interrupted his sermon with flashes of prophecy that God had given him.
There was someone among us tonight who had a bad back.
God was about to set that person free. Another person had
been out of work for many years. A job would come to them
very soon. "Those of you who have any form of sickness,"
he said, "tonight God will set you free!" I found myself listening carefully every time he prophesied, half-expecting to
hear him name my problems. *There is someone here tonight
who walked away from God long ago. Turn her around and set
her on the right path.*

As Pastor Adeboye's sermon wound to a close, the music
climbed to a crescendo. That was when he started whispering into his microphone, luring lost souls. That was the moment when he stepped on the gas. Trumpets and piano notes
guided his voice like an arrow into a place beyond the brain.
Gray-haired grandmothers began kicking off their pumps
in a Pentecostal fury and danced across the floor, children

threw up their hands to God as if they had suddenly been unshackled. Pastor Adeboye's voice sharpened and crackled and he pleaded with us all to come back to God and cast off our evil, doubting ways. He reminded us of everything the Lord had promised. The poor will be rich, the meek will inherit the earth, and the lost will be found. Those who were slighted and disrespected on earth would receive their just reward. Pastor Adeboye said that God had arrived before us at this campground and had been waiting for us. "Now the two of you are about to meet!" he shouted.

Later that night, I'd sit in my car for hours as dawn cracked open over the Texas countryside and the long, rumbling pack of cars wound their way through the dirt roads of Hunt County until they reached the interstate. Back at my motel, I'd nod to the elderly proprietor when he glared at me—no doubt a loose woman coming home from a nefarious liaison. I'd pull the blinds closed and curl up on the double bed, opening my laptop to capture all my impressions while they were still fresh on the surface of my mind. I'd write about the scene as if I was outside of it, unaffected by it.

But there in the tent, I'd watched uneasily, holding my pen tightly. I hadn't counted on the music and the way it swelled open a hollow place deep inside my chest. When people started rising around me like prairie dogs popping up out of their holes, I stayed seated until I felt a hand on my shoulder. The woman next to me, a young mother whose baby son was bound on her back in a colorful *kanga*, met my eyes and beckoned me up. My throat seized up, and I started to wave her away. But it was one-thirty in the morning, and the woman had the same sweet half-smile my mother had, so I rose obediently, my pen and notebook clattering to the floor.

She and I were two small bodies in the midst of thousands, swaying in a sea of buzzing voices. I could feel all the faith and passion that I'd had as a girl, right there beneath the surface of my skin. My brain reminded me that I didn't believe in any of this anymore, but when the music tugged at me, I didn't fight it. I lifted my face to the sky.

For the first time in years I heard the raw, raucous beauty of those strange heavenly languages, swelling to fill all the space available in that tent. I couldn't understand a word of it apart from a few scattered phrases, *Holy* and *Jesus*, but it didn't matter. I knew they were calling on the Lord in tongues, singing their love for him and calling on him to fulfill all his promises. It would have been so easy to open my mouth and join those other babbling voices in a mass of praise, but my mouth stayed closed. Instead I breathed all that frantic worship in and held it inside my rib cage. My neighbor squeezed my hand and I squeezed back. Then she lifted both our hands to the sky, as if to get a little bit closer to the place where she thought God's power was.

Chapter 12

The County

From the moment I arrived back at my parents' rented farmhouse, I could sense my father's mood like the weather. A good day and he'd be out in the backyard, fiddling with his chicken coop and fertilizing his garden. A bad one and he'd be glowering in a straight-backed chair at the end of the kitchen table, arms folded in front of him and brow furrowed. From the way my mother and my brothers tiptoed around him I'd know to stay out of the kitchen. But today was a crisp June day, and my mother said he was outside cutting boards for his chicken coop. When he limped in from the backyard to find me in the kitchen trading gossip with my mother, my father hugged me tightly, pressing my cheek against his scratchy beard, and asked me to get him a beer. I grabbed a bottle for myself as well, pouring the cold Budweiser into glasses.

"You look good, Dad," I told him, and he grunted. He knew I was being nice. Time had frosted his beard and thinned his hairline. A stroke a few years before had cut him down, gimping his right leg and slurring his speech.

Semi-retired, he whiled away the days watching television, reading crime novels, and tending his rosebushes.

My mother started pulling various covered dishes out of the fridge. She pushed two tomatoes on me, still dripping from their quick rinse at the sink, and as we made lunch she asked me to fill her in about my trip.

When I had first called my mother and told her I'd finally won a grant to travel to Nigeria, she wasn't as worried as I thought she'd be. For months I'd been telling her how whole cities in southern Nigeria shut down for church on Sunday mornings. Truck drivers frequently pasted salvation messages across the front of their cabs, and the president himself resorted to intercessory prayer when his wife became ill. My mother found these stories charming, a refreshing antidote to our increasingly secular society. She never asked me directly if I still believed, but I knew she probably assumed that my liberal arts education had wrung almost every last bit of Christianity out of me. I think she liked the idea of my spending time in a country that was so religious people didn't just ask you if you'd attended church on Sunday; they asked *which* church you attended.

My mother couldn't get an internet connection out on the farm and didn't keep up with world news, so she had no way of knowing what I'd left out in my stories about Nigeria: the massacres in Jos, the Muslim-Christian riots in Kano, the US State Department's recent ban on travel to the Niger Delta, or the recent reports of Westerners who had been nabbed by local "area boys" and held for ransom. I hadn't told my mother about the AP stringers who warned me against taking public transportation and recommended that I hire a fixer to escort me from place to place and provide security. I suspected the warnings I was getting were largely overblown, but I also had a hunch that even if my mother did know more about Nigeria, she probably wouldn't have been too worried. She had faith that God would wrap his cloud of protection around me, and she promised to pray for my safety every day. I didn't tell her not to. I didn't believe in evil spirits anymore, but on the off chance that I was wrong, my mother's prayers could only help.

As my mother busied herself over the cutting board and my father sipped his beer, I told them about the Scottish nurse who'd given me a series of vaccinations a few days ago. Apparently there was quite a bit of traffic between Houston and Lagos—oil and gas workers, mostly—so as the nurse removed the tourniquet from my arm and dabbed a drop of blood away, she told me enthusiastically all about the various troubles I'd no doubt encounter in Nigeria. First, she said, I'd have to watch out for rabid dogs. Then there was the harsh African sun. She encouraged me to bring a hat with a wide brim and some light-colored clothing that deflected the sun's harsh ultraviolet rays. I told my parents how I'd been nodding along until I realized that over the summer, Houston was typically ten degrees hotter than southern Nigeria. My mother wanted to know if she'd had any other advice for me. I told them how the nurse had suggested that I wear a fake wedding ring to fend off potential suitors, and my father guffawed.

My mother beckoned me outside, piling my arms with placemats and plates and silverware. She slowly made her way behind me, wincing because of her bad knee, and then wiped the long table on the porch clean and set it with stoneware. As she laid out freshly boiled sweet corn and salad with tender cucumbers and tomatoes, I looked out over the yard.

A hunched willow tree swept the lawn with its branches, and the fat Persian cat that my mother rescued a few years back hunted voles and mice in the unmown grass. But the real beauty was in the riot of color that was my father's garden. A hundred or so potted plants dotted the rim of the wide southern porch. He planted jasmine and gardenias for their sweet, lingering scent; brilliant blue puff-ball hydrangeas; gawky, overeager black-eyed Susans; savory herbs; and the delicate peonies my mother loved. His trees were all in five-gallon buckets with holes drilled in the bottom, so he could take them with him when they had to move again.

Years ago, when I was away at college, Sam had started sneaking cigarettes after my parents had gone to bed. One morning my father had found a cigarette butt in one of his prized gardenia pots, and he went on a rampage, knocking his beloved plants off the wide porch and onto the ground. He didn't stop until all the plants were upended, and then he took off in his truck. My mother shut herself up in her bedroom and prayed for deliverance, but Joshua went out onto the porch and just stood there for a long time. He must have been eleven then, and I suppose he started with what was closest to him, righting the pots that were still whole, consolidating the plants whose pots had shattered, sweeping and raking spilled soil into manageable piles.

I remembered talking to Joshua the next day on the phone as I squatted on the stairs of the old pink house I was renting at the time. "I lost some," he said. "The jasmine is just not gonna make it."

Who knows where my father slept that night—his truck, maybe—but when he came home sometime in the late morning, he sat in the cab for a while. The view from the driveway is such that he must have seen the porch just before he lumbered up the hill to the house, stopping to feel the leaves of a hearty tomato bush that had made it through the previous day's drama without being much worse for wear. When he finally opened the screen door, he looked at my mother, who shook her head, and then at my two oldest brothers, who refused to meet his eyes. I wasn't there to see the look on Joshua's face when my father came in, but my mother told me he was sitting on the couch, reading *Architectural Digest*. I guess my father reached for him, to hug him, maybe, or thank him for putting things in order. But Joshua looked up and shrugged. "I didn't do it for you," he said. "I just like plants."

ᵂ

I asked my mother where Joshua was, and she told me he was at church. I wrinkled my nose. "Really? It's Saturday."

"Didn't I tell you?" she said. "He's started going to this little church north of the county. He's there all weekend. They have a Bible study thing every Saturday. And the pastor is Nigerian!"

Maybe I should have been surprised, but instead it seemed to confirm what I already suspected—that Nigerian evangelists were about to take the United States by storm. I told my mother how I'd opened the Sunday *New York Times* the other day to find a feature article about the Redeemed Church. The reporter even quoted Rev. Bart Pierce, who pastored Rock Church of Baltimore and had been leading the dedication service the day I first decided to leave the church. He said that Africans would be the midwives for the next great move of God in America. My mother asked why that was, and I unpacked it as best as I knew how. Westerners used to think they had a kind of monopoly on Christianity, but that was changing fast. Scholars predicted that in another fifteen years, a quarter of all Christians would live in Africa—and most of them would be Pentecostal. Some even traced the roots of Pentecostalism past Azusa Street or that moment when that girl in Kansas City first spoke in tongues, all the way to the Southern plantations where West African slaves infused traditional beliefs into their practice of Christianity. Perhaps the Pentecostal faith was actually born in Nigeria. My mother wasn't convinced, and I understood why. There was something almost dangerous about the idea that the way we worshipped had an origin, a history—and something even more threatening about the idea that "heathen" practices had rubbed off on Christianity.

As we ate, my mother started catching me up on all the gossip I had missed. I barely remembered the ponytailed girls I grew up with, but my mother told me that most of them had stayed close to home. Miss Kathy's daughter was living over in the Ranch Club now. Two of Pastor Jim's daughters had families of their own, as did Liz and Karen, as did Chacie. And then my mother stopped short, like she was remembering something, and her eyes flickered down to the scratched linoleum. In an odd, clipped voice and a slight stutter she told me that we lost Molly. At first I couldn't place the name. And then I remembered the twins and our long ago walks on the beach with my father. My mother was still talking when I snapped back into the conversation. Molly had struggled with addiction. To what my mother wasn't sure—most likely Oxy or heroin. She'd died in March, just a few months ago. Her parents had buried her in Saint John's Holiness cemetery on Hallowing Point Road. She was twenty-nine years old, just a month older than me.

I hadn't thought of Molly in years. I remembered that she'd had a son when we were both in high school, a little boy who had died shortly after he was born. I asked my mother about Molly's sister Emmy. My mother said that she seemed to be doing well—she lived across the bridge in Lexington Park and had a few little boys of her own. My mother mentioned her boyfriend's name and a vague memory surfaced from Facebook of a goateed man with a beer-swollen face. A county boy.

❧

After dinner we sat around for a little while in the living room, talking half-heartedly while my father watched an Arnold Schwarzenegger movie. I told her about the guy I'd just started dating, a tall, lean scientist with a shock of frizzy hair and an aquiline nose. Our backgrounds couldn't have been more different. Jake was raised by a pair of liberal psychotherapists, and their Pennsylvania home was full of blond wood, plants, musical instruments, and multiple varieties of herbal tea. They had taught Jake that no feeling was intrinsically bad—it was how you chose to respond to those feelings that mattered. Now Jake was a neuroscientist who cultivated a healthy sense of awe at the way chance and accident had collided with natural law to result in the world we knew. He was gentle and kind, and laughed so often that he had permanent wrinkles under his eyes. Being with him soothed me in some deep sense. I suspected that he didn't quite understand what drew me to Nigeria, but he supported the trip, even offering to help wire me money from my US bank account if my ATM card didn't work while I was there.

My mother smiled and patted my hand. "He sounds nice," she said. "Is he a Christian?"

I squirmed and told her that Jake was raised Quaker, which wasn't quite true. He had gone to a Quaker high school, though, and his parents sometimes attended Quaker meetings. His father even carried a little card in his wallet that read, "In case of emergency, please be silent."

My mother nodded, satisfied that at least I was dating a man, and at least he wasn't a total heathen. She asked more about my life in Houston, and I rattled on about my professors and the friends I'd made. As the conversation stopped and started, I became aware of a faint, slippery shape between us, the ghost of the woman I could have been. She looked like me—messy ponytail at a precarious angle—but she had a fat blond baby on her lap and a toddler leaning against her thigh. She was a stranger to the world of graduate school, of copy machines and laser printers, of meetings and deadlines. She and my mother were natural confidantes. The woman's toddler was up late with an earache, but my mother's suggestion about a hot bath worked wonders. They traded stories about the day, made plans for a birthday party. Their houses were close enough that they could drop off things from the grocery store that had been purchased two for one, on sale. But instead my mother was stuck with me, nodding at my stories in a distracted way and not asking questions. When she offered me some chocolate, I said no, and when she rose to get some for herself, I checked my phone.

Lately I'd been trading emails with a man named Gary Foxcroft, a British aid officer who worked primarily in Nigeria. Gary had been doing research in the Niger Delta state of Akwa Ibom—pronounced *Ah-qway-bomb*, the two words running together with a glottal thrust—when he had come across a strange phenomenon in which Pentecostal pastors in the area were accusing children of practicing witchcraft. Often the children came from families who had experienced hardship: the death of a family member, unemployment, or some other calamity. Their mother and father would bring them to a local church, and often the pastor would confirm their suspicions. Sometimes the child would be tied up for days outside the church while the pastor prayed over them and tried to starve the spirits out of them. Sometimes, when the pastor finally released them, their families wouldn't want them anymore, and the children were on their own.

Gary had started a nonprofit organization to help the children and had recently been profiled in a documentary put together by a pair of Dutch filmmakers. The premiere was in a few days in New York, and Gary had wrangled a ticket for me. Since I'd first heard about the children in the Delta, I hadn't been able to stop thinking about them. I think it had something to do with how, as a child, I had nodded along with the rest of the congregation as Pastor Jim paced the length of the altar, waving his leather-bound Bible and calling out curses on nonbelievers and blessings on those who did God's will. If that man had told our congregation to sell everything we owned and move to southern Nigeria, I think we would have done it. I wasn't sure what we would have done if he had said that somewhere among us there was a child with an evil spirit inside him that could only be driven out through force. I have a feeling we might have parted like a sea and left the child alone to face whatever might have awaited him.

⟡

Joshua finally came home close to ten o'clock. He grinned at the sight of me on the couch and reached down for a hug.

It had been a while since I'd been home, and since then his hair had darkened and curled and he'd grown longer and leaner, until he was just taller than me. He had blue eyes and a little bit of scruff on his lip. He was scrawny but stylish, wearing skinny jeans and expensive sneakers and well-fitted shirts in brighter colors than boys could have gotten away with when I was in high school. He'd always had eclectic interests as a kid, ordering books on hotel management and real estate development, buying and selling coins from professional dealers and driving hard bargains. Like the rest of my brothers, he could fix a leaky pipe, lay a patio, put shingles on a roof, hang crown molding, do tile work, and install a transmission on a truck. He was patient with my father and always there in the midst of whatever drama my brothers and I were causing, a steady and reliable force. My mother had told me that he had recently fallen in love with a blond girl who worked at Safeway. She'd been going to church with him.

Joshua and I sat on the couch for a little while and talked a bit, but it was late and I was tired from my flight. My mother had volunteered his room to me, and he agreed to sleep on the couch. I hugged him goodnight and once I was upstairs, I spent a while looking around his room. On the wall above his bed was a color-coded map from the International Mission Board that showed all the unreached people around the world. North America was blue, which meant they had been exposed to the Lord, and Africa was a mix of green and red and yellow. On the whiteboard on the wall at the foot of Joshua's bed was a list of his goals: go to community college, then apply to the University of Maryland, then get a pilot's license and start his own business. And in his scrawled handwriting: "Do things God's way, and you won't need a Plan B." A stack of Bibles and a thesaurus were piled on his nightstand, and I imagined him poring over words late into the night, trying to shake meaning out of those centuries-old verses, meaning that was applicable to his life today. Next to the Bibles were lists of names and places, on loose-leaf paper in pencil. Prayer lists. I remember when I had those lists as well.

The morning before I left, my father woke me up early to drive over to Fast-Stop, the little convenience store and gas station near the highway. They had a few picnic tables out by the propane tanks and dumpsters where teenagers gathered to smoke in the evenings, and where my father chatted with his sister in the mornings over coffee, if they weren't in one of their legendary year-long fights. My father went inside to order his coffee, and the cashier—a slight woman my age, with a thick brown braid—flashed him a smile that showed her braces and greeted him by name, then grabbed his preferred brand of chewing tobacco from the shelf above her without him saying a word. On the picnic table we sipped burnt-tasting, lukewarm coffee from paper cups while my father picked his teeth with a toothpick and nodded to the pickup trucks that rumbled by the gas station.

§

Whenever I visited, I felt like I was going back in time, funneling back to an America I didn't think much about anymore. An America of fields and farms and barns and clapboard churches, where children said *yes ma'am* and *no ma'am*, where strangers greeted each other with a nod in the grocery stores, where chances were that every stranger you met had some relation in common with someone you already knew. But to build a happy life and be accepted in this county, you had to accept a number of irrefutable truths. Good people voted Republican, the party of family values, and went to church on Sunday. When women had children, they quit their jobs and stayed home like the mothers they were meant to be. Men belonged with women and women with men. Everyone seemed to share the belief that the country was on a downward spiral and only prayer and divine intervention would set things right again.

My father nodded at one of the men walking into Fast-Stop, a beefy man in a camouflage jacket. He looked vaguely familiar, and my father told me he'd attended Rock Church with us a long time ago and had come across hard times since then. It seemed harder than ever to make it in the county, if you were poor. The wealthy and middle class were doing just fine with their big houses overlooking the water, but the poor were struggling—whether or not they stayed faithful. There weren't many opportunities here, just jobs at Walmart or the fast-food restaurants. And all the new houses in the county were priced so that only the commuters could afford them. I told my father it was good that he and my mom still had the farm, where they got a good deal on the rent because no one else would be willing to send their cars down that washed-out driveway every day. But my father twiddled his toothpick between his fingers and said they'd see how long that would last. Their landlord was an old man with a bad heart, and his wife was pushing him to sell the farm while he could still handle all the arrangements himself. I stewed on that news for a while before finally tapping my wrist and telling my father I needed to get going. I was heading up to New York later that afternoon for the premiere of the documentary, and I needed to drop off my rental car in DC before catching the bus.

We packed into my father's truck and exited onto that rutted-out dirt road for the final drive back to the farm. When we reached the house and my mother hugged me goodbye, the farm was still on my mind. I wanted to ask my mother what they'd do if the landlord sold the land, but instead I said something about how they were lucky to have what they did in this market, and how I was hoping they'd get to hang onto the house for a while.

"The Lord will provide for us," my mother said lightly. "He always has. Don't worry so much." But when she answered that way my own heart hardened. I nodded, disappointed. She and my father had been faithful for over thirty years, tithing a tenth of their income to the church, doing their best to follow God's commandments, but there was no reward in sight. For her, that was what it meant to be faithful. To me it just seemed irresponsible. My mother smiled at me again and reached out to tuck a loose strand of hair behind my ear. I flinched, not used to being touched.

※

The premiere of *Saving Africa's Witch Children* was held a block from Bryant Park at the HBO headquarters. It was mostly attended by NGO types and activists, the kind who were overly enthusiastic about the pre-screening spread, which included tiny crystal glasses of gazpacho and bacon-wrapped scallops. When the bell summoned us, we packed into a small auditorium, sized for the premieres of similar foreign political documentaries such as *China's Stolen Children*, *Afghan Star*, and *Burma VJ: Reporting from a Closed Country*.

The film was produced by two Dutch journalists, a husband–and–wife team who looked like rock stars with their shaggy hair and leather jackets. They had filmed deliverance ceremonies, interviewed villagers who had cast out children for being witches, and followed the footsteps of two main characters—the wiry, gap-toothed British aid worker Gary Foxcroft and Sam Itauma, a tall, broadly built man from Akwa Ibom who had built a relief center for the children.

The film chronicled the story of one young girl who was accused of being a witch after her mother died. She had a shaved head, thin arms and legs, and her belly was fat from malnutrition or parasites. Sam and Gary came across her in a market wearing a dirty pink T-shirt, shaking with fear after a gang of young men had confronted her and told her to leave. They took her to the center that Sam had built on his land and then, after some time, tried unsuccessfully to reunite her with her family. The film's villain was Helen Ukpabio, a deliverance preacher headquartered in the nearby state of Calabar. In the YouTube videos I'd seen, she was a stocky woman with a deep voice, inclined toward wide-brimmed hats in jewel tones and pumps dyed to match. Helen claimed that when she was fourteen, she was initiated into the ways of witchcraft and was even betrothed to Lucifer himself. God delivered her, and now she could look at someone for just a moment and know if the person was walking in the light of God or was plagued by spirits of poverty, infertility, and disease. My father, who worshipped the same God Helen worshipped, would have called this the gift of discernment.

In Helen's sermons and books, she unveiled the mysteries of witchcraft, telling stories of people who went traveling and begged water from strangers only to have spirits creep into them. Once possessed, they themselves became witches and brought sin and destruction wherever they went, unless they were stopped by a man or woman of God like herself. Helen believed that when it comes to witchcraft, not even children would be spared. One of her books gave a set of instructions for identifying witches under the age of two: "If a child . . . screams in the night, cries and is always feverish with deteriorating health, he or she is a servant of Satan." When the Dutch filmmakers recorded Helen secretly in one of her churches, she became angry and denied that there were any children being tortured in the churches of Akwa Ibom. It was Sam Itauma who was the real villain, she said. He was out for money for that orphanage of his and willing to tell any kind of lie to get it.

After the screening, the filmmakers, along with Gary and Sam, took questions and comments from the audience. Sam wore a black suit with a gold tie, looking a bit like a megachurch pastor. Gary had closely cropped hair and was dressed more informally, in khakis and a button-down shirt. Everyone was up in arms that the evil being done in Akwa Ibom was being done in the name of God. One young woman with long hair and a peasant-style blouse leapt out of her chair the moment that the Q&A began. "It's just not Christian!" she said. "It's not biblical! What's happening is a total perversion of the Bible. It's an affront to Christian principles!"

I sat a few rows behind her, but even from there I had the woman pegged as Methodist or Presbyterian. She had probably grown up in one of those mainstream denominations that Pastor Jim had scorned, saying that they were so beholden to their bylaws and their board of directors that they forgot to be beholden to God. Her people were probably descendants of those European missionaries who had poured into West Africa after the abolition of the slave

trade, scorning indigenous religions as primitive and superstitious, and building schools to teach children that demons
and spirits didn't actually exist. I understood the point she
was trying to make, but it was hard for me to accept her
claim that there was nothing Christian about Helen Ukpabio's teachings. In my recollection the Bible was chock full
of demons.

In the book of Exodus, the Lord told Moses that witches
must be put to death. In Matthew, Jesus himself cast demons out of a man and sent them into a herd of pigs, who
ran themselves off the edge of a cliff. Years later Paul tells
Christians to put on the whole armor of God, so they can
wrestle against principalities and powers, against the rulers
of the darkness and the spiritual hosts of wickedness. And
there was that story about the time when Moses's brother,
Aaron, found himself in a face-off with Pharaoh's sorcerers.
He threw his staff to the ground and it turned into a snake,
wriggling and writhing. The sorcerers tried to scare him by
throwing their own staffs to the ground, and those staffs
turned into snakes as well. But because Aaron's staff was
blessed by God, his snake was far bigger than the sorcerers'
snakes, and it consumed them. That story was a favorite of
my father's—as was any biblical story that featured a battle
to the death between the spirits of darkness and the forces
of light. It reminded him that we served a God who made
demons tremble.

As the filmmakers began expounding on Helen Ukpabio's perversion of Christianity, I thought of my father back
in the kitchen of that farmhouse in southern Maryland where
I'd left him, drinking his coffee and reading the *Washington
Post*. I knew that if I sat down at the table with him and
asked him if he believed in the spirit world, he would put

down his paper, cross his arms, and say yes, without a doubt. We live in the natural world and have become accustomed to its laws, but that doesn't mean those laws cannot be broken. That was the miracle of Jesus, he'd say. They killed him and he rose again and showed that not even death could hold him back. We can't afford to forget that the world is throbbing and pulsing with spirits, and our only defense against them is to keep ourselves pure and free from sin.

If I leaned in and asked if someone could be possessed by an evil spirit, he might say he'd seen it with his own eyes, and that spirits are not what you might think. Forget about witches on brooms with pointy hats. Think instead of the spirit of stubbornness, the spirit of fear, the spirit of defeat. Think of a dark feeling that comes on slowly, a spirit inside you that says you are nothing, worse than nothing, that there is something evil and bad within you. Think of the way that worry bubbles up deep in your belly and warps your thinking, telling you that life will always be full of pain and trouble. If you listen to that voice you could be led astray. You could succumb to sickness and disease and even death.

I imagined that if I asked my father if a child could be possessed by a spirit, he might squint and try to gauge my motives. Then he'd remind me that in Exodus 20, God told us himself that he was a jealous God, and he would not tolerate the worship of any other God before him. If he was disobeyed, then the sins of the father would be visited on the children, up until the third and fourth generations. If I argued that the punishment was too harsh, my father might flash a crooked smile. I was young and hadn't seen very much of the world yet. It made sense that I could still tell myself that all children were born innocent, that demons weren't real. That God was all sweetness and light, and not jealous or vindictive. Maybe I'd forgotten how the Lord cast Adam and Eve out of paradise, how he once drowned the entire earth in a fit of anger and spared only Noah and those who had taken up residence on his ark. How the Lord had once sent an angel to test Abraham by telling him to bind up and sacrifice his only son. How God had tortured his beloved servant Job just to make a point. How God sat silently by and allowed his own son to be nailed to a cross, a crown of thorns pressed upon the tender flesh of his forehead, his sides pierced with swords.

Our God was a God of great power and great authority, and the world danced on his axis, not our own. If I had forgotten all of that, then it was no wonder I'd also forgotten that the Devil's agents were everywhere among us, scratching and crawling at our edges, searching for a way to get inside.

Chapter 13

Beloved, Feel Free

Beloved, the moist Xeroxed form implored me, *feel free to give accurate and complete information.*

That injunction, like so many I received during the weeks I spent in Nigeria, was loving but commanding, half demand and half suggestion. The questions were simple, and yet a certain shrewdness belied their order, as if the author demanded increasingly concrete evidence to back up the responses.

> *Are you a Christian (Yes/No)?*
> *When did you accept the Lord Jesus Christ? Give testimony of your salvation.*
> *Do you believe every word in the Holy Bible?*
> *Are you baptized by immersion in water (Yes/No) . . . If yes, when?*
> *Are you baptized in the Holy Ghost with evidence of speaking in tongues (Yes/No)?*

The answers to these questions made me a lukewarm Christian at best, but even if I said yes to all of them, I knew

more were sure to follow. *Do you read your Bible every day?*
No. I didn't even bring one to Nigeria. *Do you evangelize?*
Not a chance. *Do you indulge in cultic activity?* I read my horo-
scope faithfully. *Do you smoke?* Sometimes, to the dismay of
my faculty sponsor. *Drink?* Yes. *Use the Lord's name in vain?*
Yes. *Swear?* Yes. *Gossip?* Yes. *Engage in sexual immorality?*
Yes. That was the thing about Pentecostals. It wasn't enough
to simply believe or to go to church on Sundays. After you
accepted the Lord into your heart, you then had to demonstrate your beliefs on a daily basis, becoming purer and holier
by the day. Becoming a Christian meant leaving your old self
behind and being recreated in the image of God.

Beside me, my friend Bukke pinched her mouth into
a smile. She was a tall woman in her early twenties, and
the long braids framing her face swayed in the breeze of
the outdoor amphitheater. She patted my shoulder and
told me to take my time. I knew it wouldn't do any good
to try to get out of filling out the form by reminding her
that I wasn't a typical visitor. Back in Houston I'd written
a grant proposal that used words like "methodology" and
"participant-observation" and "fieldwork." I proposed a two-
month research trip to Nigeria, where I would interview
believers and collect their testimonies while also studying
the history of Pentecostal Christianity. I left Houston with
a suitcase full of notebooks and recording devices and a
hard drive packed with articles from journals like the *International Bulletin of Missionary Research* and the *Journal
of Religion and American Culture*. I imagined that I'd come
back from Nigeria with reams of notes and transcripts of
interviews, and then I'd synthesize all those notes and write
a dissertation that answered the question I'd posed in my
grant proposal: Was the faith of my childhood actually born

in West Africa, from the same Yorùbá rootstock as Santería and Voodoo?

But since arriving in Nigeria I'd had a difficult time getting traction on that question. I'd interviewed several professors of religion at the University of Ibadan, the oldest university in Nigeria, who shook their heads dismissively when I brought up the various ways that indigenous beliefs seemed to play out in Nigerian Pentecostal churches. Only one professor, Dr. Jegede, agreed that Pentecostalism had something in common with traditional beliefs.

"What's in African Traditional Religion that's not in Pentecostalism?" the stately professor asked me. "Nothing! There's laying on of hands—we Yorùbá believe that the forehead is the real head, not the back of your head. So when the pastor touches you, the power flows through your forehead into your whole body. There's speaking in tongues. There's money—you bring money, I give you God. If you go to an Obàtálá festival in Ife, you would never think you were in any place but the church."

When I had first shown up at his door to ask if he might have time for a few questions, Dr. Jegede settled back in his chair and made himself comfortable, starting at the very beginning. He explained that long before the missionaries came to what is now southern Nigeria, the *babalawos*—the fathers of the mysteries—were the ones who courted the spirits and shades. They guarded the great abyss separating the living and the dead, marching its steep edges in masks and feathers, hollering warnings to tricky spirits who dared to creep close to the living, making sacrifices to appease the gods, singing praise-chants to the supreme creator, Olodumare, the sky father Sàngó, and the divine couple, Obàtálá and Yemòó.

"Nowadays," Dr. Jegede continued, "if you are barren, you go to the Pentecostal church on Sunday, you bring baby clothes. You give money and you pray and you will get many children. That's original Africanism. The traditional missionary enterprise—the British kind—says if you are barren, you should go to the doctor—not the church!"

Dr. Jegede's office was on the top floor of a four-story walk-up. Meanwhile, professors of biblical studies and Christian ethics had ground-floor, air-conditioned offices in a neighboring office building with its own generator, as well as elaborate titles, job security, and fawning graduate students. Dr. Jegede complained to me that in all his years of teaching African Traditional Religion, he had only had one PhD student, and when he tried to encourage students to take his courses, they shrank back, telling him that they didn't want to go to hell.

In all my other interviews with professors and pastors, the people I spoke to politely dodged my questions about the history of the Pentecostal church. They'd share their own testimonies, but when I talked about the history of the megachurches or brought up traditional practices, they didn't have much to say. Their next question was always the same. *What about you—are you right with God?* It was a question I didn't want to answer.

This wasn't just the case in my interviews, but also in conversations with taxi drivers, the government official who stamped my visa, even the security guards at my dormitory. On my flight over to Nigeria, I'd met an elderly couple—a stern-looking woman who wore a head wrap and a gentle-faced man with wiry gray hair. They introduced themselves as Pastor and Mrs. Afolabi. Pastor Afolabi explained that he had once been a tenured professor of psychology at the University of Ibadan, but at the age of thirty-five he met Jesus and decided to give up his field entirely. He left his prestigious position at the university and went to seminary in order to better serve the Lord. "I was a psychologist," he said, "but now I'm a Christologist!" He had no choice, he explained. Psychology was all about the mind and body. Never the spirit. Never the soul. He laughed at the idea of trying to understand human behavior apart from God. God had rewarded his sacrifice, and Pastor Afolabi ended up spending the rest of his career at a thriving Baptist church on the same plot of land where the Afolabis now lived in retirement.

Just past two in the morning, as we yawned next to each other at the gate in the Atlanta airport, Mrs. Afolabi asked me if I was a Christian. I knew what she was asking: *Are you a good person? Can I trust you?* I hedged and then answered yes, ignoring the unsettled feeling that rose up in me when I said those words. The typical Christian testimony was one of being lost, then found. But my own testimony ran backward. I had been found once, but somewhere along the way I had gotten lost.

〜

Bukke and I had first met at the University of Ibadan library. I'd been transcribing my interview notes when she pulled up a chair beside my study carrel and asked me where I was from and what I was doing here. When I'd explained that I was researching the Yorùbá roots of Pentecostal Christianity she furrowed her brow, but when I added that I'd be heading to Lagos the following week to visit Redemption Camp, she squealed with delight and clasped my hands in hers. Then she took me back to her dorm room and she and her room-mate made me *egusi* soup on a hotplate.

The power had been out for several days at the university, so we sat eating in the half-darkness, lit by the faintly purple light of the dashiki cloth that wavered in the wind of the window. As we ate, street noise filtered in: the sputtering of the *okadas*, the motorbikes that ferried students and staff around the sprawling University of Ibadan campus for less than a nickel; the sound of someone hacking at the grass outside with a rusty machete; the swishing sound from a broom as an elderly woman crab-walked across the court-yard, sweeping leaves away with a small handle-less brush. Nearby, children shrieked with delight, playing clapping games near their families' carts while their parents hawked cheap spiral-bound notebooks or ears of spiced corn.

Bukke and her roommate Titi were both members of the Redeemed Church, and as I ate they talked over each other, narrating the mythical history of the church. It was a story that I knew well. The pastor who founded the church had once had a vision of a blackboard bearing the English words: "The Redeemed Christian Church of God." He couldn't read or write—in any language—but miraculously he managed to write the words down. Shortly after that, the Lord made a covenant with him. God told the pastor that he would provide for the church as long as its members would serve the Lord faithfully and obediently. God also told him that when Jesus finally returned, he would meet the church in all his glory.

I told Bukke and Titi about a book I'd been reading by a pastor named Leo Bawa. He called Nigeria the trigger of Africa. He pointed out that if you pivoted the continent

counter-clockwise ninety degrees, so South Africa rests
against India, then the shape of Africa looks like a gun with
southern Nigeria serving as the trigger. Bawa wanted to see
Nigerians carry the gospel to other African nations first, and
then, once those souls were won, the gun could fire off missionaries from Africa to win the world for Christ. "God will
use Africa," Bawa said, "the downtrodden and overlooked
Continent, to usher in the King."

They nodded and smiled. They knew there were some
good Christians in America—"Joel Osteen!" Titi chimed
in—but for the most part they assumed we'd become a heathen nation. When I told Bukke and Titi about my childhood in the church, dancing and clapping and speaking
in tongues, they were amazed. Titi in particular seemed
doubtful. "You danced?" she said, trying hard to imagine
white people being touched by the Spirit.

Bukke and Titi were thrilled that I'd visited the Redeemed Church in Houston and had attended the convention, but they weren't at all surprised. They believed, as Leo
Bawa did, that Nigerians had a divine mandate to save fallen
Westerners, and they shared Pastor Fadele's conviction that
my visit to Redemption Camp would be life-changing. Each
of them regularly made the long pilgrimage south to attend
the services, and Titi tried hard to explain what was so special about the church.

"It used to be the bush," Titi told me. "Truly wild. There
were apes and snakes everywhere. And then the church
came in and cut all the trees down and built the most beautiful houses. You will see. So quiet and peaceful! The light
always works and the toilets flush. And when the preaching starts . . . !" She got so excited that she almost burned
the soup.

When I told Hannah, a German instructor who lived on my hall, that I'd accepted Bukke's invitation to attend the Redeemed Church student fellowship on Sunday morning, she rolled her eyes and tossed her shiny blond hair. "These Nigerians and their churches . . . ," she said. "When they ask me to go with them, I say I am busy worshipping Satan."

I suppressed a smile thinking of the temper tantrum that Hannah had thrown last Sunday around seven in the morning, when a lone man—from the look of him, a graduate student—took it upon himself to set up a megaphone and a makeshift pulpit to conduct a solo church service, aimed up at the dorm rooms on the second floor of Balewa Hall. With approximately one in three Nigerians in the south identifying as Pentecostal, the reaction of most of my dormitory-mates was praise. They praised the lone man for being a witness, even if it cost them a few hours of sleep. Hannah was the lone holdout. Long after the man had packed up, she stood in the hallway in her bathrobe telling anyone who would listen how inappropriate his performance had been.

I'd been in the southern city of Ibadan for three weeks now and unlike Hannah, I'd made a habit of saying yes to every invitation I got. As early as five-thirty in the morning, the open-air auditoriums and cafeterias in the middle of each dormitory would start throbbing with song, drums, and sometimes trumpets, waking me to strains of Yorùbá songs I didn't understand, and other hymns I remember my mother singing as she washed dishes. By eight o'clock on the Sunday morning that I was supposed to meet Bukke, I'd hit snooze three times, hauled water from the pump in front of my dormitory, gasped my way through a cold-water

bucket shower, and mixed up a strong cup of Sanka after
heating water on my kerosene stove. As I waited for Bukke
and Titi at the edge of the parking lot, I heard the strains of
Pentecostal worship songs once again.

Ibadan was a major city, but it had a sleepy feel compared
to the thriving metropolis of Lagos, a few hours to the south.
Even so, my fellow students at the University of Ibadan had
endless choices for which church to attend. I counted approximately thirty-five different options on campus and
another seventy or so within a five-minute walk of the campus gates. Posters advertising services hung at every corner. One could attend the ecumenical Christian Chapel of
the Resurrection, the lively Assemblies of God church, the
miracle-based God Will Do It Ministries, the student fellowship for Mountain of Fire and Miracles, the somewhat
traditional Precious Stones Society, the white-garment African Independent Churches—the list went on and on.

Bukke and Titi picked me up in a minivan and we drove
a few miles to a kind of worship park on the south side of
the campus, a series of large open-structures with red roofs,
concrete floors, and electricity hookups for microphones and
large electric fans. The services usually followed the same
schedule, and Bukke's student fellowship was no different.
First there was praise and worship, then the testimonies,
then the tithes and offering, and then the sermon. Just before the final prayer the pastor surveyed the congregation
and asked if there was anyone who was attending service for
the first time. He politely ignored me, as if there was a veil
over my white skin. When I stood up, he started as if he was
seeing me for the first time, and the congregation exploded
into applause.

The drummer and piano player broke out into a rendition of a jazzy traditional song with an English chorus: *Welcome, friend / Welcome, friend.* Then I was handed around for handshakes and hugs. Bukke gathered my things for me and directed me to the back of the church, where I signed my name in a ledger. With all the services I attended I was used to being given welcome cards to fill out with my name and contact information, and I'd become spoiled by the boxes of fruit juice and packets of cookies that were handed out to new faces. But this was the first time that the welcome card took up a whole sheet of paper, and the first time it had such a personal tone.

Bukke rummaged in her purse for a pencil and directed me into a plastic chair at the back of the open-air sanctuary. As she and Titi stacked up plastic chairs alongside the pastor, I finally started filling out the form, beginning with the easiest question. *When did you accept the Lord Jesus Christ?* At the age of five, sitting on my mother's knee. "I believe," I'd whispered, because Jesus felt as real as California, as my aunt Marilyn's postcards of palm trees and oceans and dolphins and all those other fantastic things that I hadn't yet seen but which definitely still existed. My mother had cried with gladness and recorded the date of my confession in lovely scrolling letters in her olive-green Bible, next to the date of my birth. My mother said that God had his own book up in heaven, and when it was time for us to go back there, he'd run his hands down its pages until he found our names, and then the pearly gates would be opened for us. It was so easy it felt like I was getting away with something. All I had to do was believe, and then I would be saved from hellfire. God would hold us close to his heart, and even when we died we'd still be together in heaven. What God has written, my mother told me, no man can erase.

Do you believe every word of the Holy Bible? No, but I wrote yes anyway. I thought back to the first Bible that was my very own, the one I'd gotten when I was ten, the Precious Moments edition complete with pen-and-ink sketches of bobble-headed, doe-eyed children lying down with lions and lambs. I was taught to treat that book with respect. God wrote it, my mother cautioned me, through the hands of many men. That Bible was only ink and paper, with a white pleather cover and a glued binding, but I was taught to never put that book on the ground.

When I got to the question about water baptism, the memories flooded back, thick and fast: The maroon choir robe, the chemical taste of the chlorinated water, the pastor's heavy hand resting on my back. The crowd of people just behind my parents, lifting their hands in my direction, praying that I would be blessed with God's favor and kept safe from the Evil One.

There was a clatter as the pastor secured a tarp and a padlock over the A/V equipment, and it broke up my reverie. I could see Bukke and Titi waiting for me over near the car park. It was long past lunchtime, and I needed to walk over to the market to pick up some rice and tomato sauce before heading back to Balewa Hall. I hoped that Hannah and our friend Efi would be home as well so we could all eat together.

Are you baptized in the Holy Ghost with evidence of speaking in tongues? It was the final question, and I answered yes. Despite all my talk about ethnography and fieldwork, despite my doubts and lapses, I had started to wonder if it might be possible to believe again. Since arriving in Nigeria, I found myself murmuring prayers and thumbing through the small green Bible that I'd bought from a street vendor at the market just outside the university's gates. I was falling into that old familiar way of thinking, the same way that I felt my syllables melting and lengthening when I came home to Maryland after a long time away. I thought maybe that old Holy Ghost language might still be wedged inside me somewhere after all, sleeping like a baby, waiting for the moment when I was no longer ashamed to let it out of my mouth.

In a way it would be a relief to speak in that language again. It would be like choosing sides. I'd be casting my lot with the poor and disinherited, those left behind by a cold and calculating capitalist economy. I'd be claiming the inheritance of William Seymour, the half-blind preacher who led a hardscrabble band of believers to revival on Azusa Street. I'd be sitting beside Bukke and Titi as they worshipped a God who was a gift to the world from the Yorùbá people, a God who seemed as indigenous to this country as pounded yam or talking drums. I'd be standing on their side and the side of my parents, casting off worldly concerns, the jargon of my grant proposal, and everyone who chased after worldly sensation or fame and reputation over all the things that really mattered.

There was only one problem—I didn't believe in that God anymore. But part of me was so intrigued by the prospect of believing again that that problem seemed surmountable. Maybe I just needed to get closer, like Pastor Fadele had recommended. I needed to stand with a million other worshippers at the annual Holy Ghost Service at Redemption Camp and feel the power of God all around me. Maybe then my doubts would shrivel up under the weight of all that praise. And so I went back to the top of the form and tested out that language, writing *yes, I am a Christian.*

❧ *Chapter 14* ❧

Trigger of Africa

"Christianity is about power," Pastor Shola told me when I first met him. "When I have the power from God, I become a prince, a king." By day Pastor Shola was the head of the maintenance department at the University of Ibadan, but on nights and weekends he served as a pastor in the Redeemed Church. Pastor Shola was far more in demand than Dr. Jegede was—his multiple cell phones rang off the hook with requests from parishioners, his supervisor at the university, and higher-ups in the church. He continually promised them all that things would be resolved in one hour's time. He seemed to be a modern-day *babalawo*, only he looked to the Bible for answers instead of divining the future from cowrie shells or palm nuts.

I told Pastor Shola that I was trying to figure out how to get from Ibadan to Lagos for the monthly Holy Ghost Service at Redemption Camp, and he laughed delightedly at the way the Lord worked. He and his family were going as well. And when he learned that I'd been planning to make the trip in a *danfo*—one of the old Volkswagen minibuses whose trips had such a high fatality rate that passengers had to fill out a form identifying their next of kin before they climbed aboard—he immediately offered me a spot in their minivan.

When Pastor Shola picked me up outside Balewa Hall, I was startled at the sight of him. Instead of his threadbare Western suit, he wore an agbada of the brightest fabric I had ever seen—a mix of lime-green and orange and red and gold. He introduced me to his wife and three children, all clad in the same fabric.

On the way to Lagos the Sholas told me more about Redemption Camp. They said that the monthly Holy Ghost Services typically drew between eighty thousand and a hundred thousand people, but there would be ten times as many people attending the annual convention in August. Tonight's service ran from 7 p.m. to 3 a.m., at which time most of the congregants stretched out on the long wooden benches in the covered outdoor amphitheater and slept until the first light, when it was safe to be on the roads again.

      ❧

When we stopped at a police checkpoint fifty miles outside of Ibadan, everyone sat up a little straighter, saying a quick prayer that these were honorable policemen and not the robbing types. Pastor Shola explained that the checkpoints ostensibly existed to monitor the roads and prevent carjacking or armed robbery, but much of the time the police themselves were the threat. The drivers of *danfos* got the worst of it. Most glided through the checkpoints with *dash*—a green N20 or blue N50 note clenched in their fists for an easy handoff. Private drivers weren't immune to shakedowns either. Pastor Shola said that every so often there was a news briefing about a driver who was shot when he hit the gas at a police checkpoint to avoid paying. The checkpoint wasn't the only harrowing part of the journey. On the Lagos-Ibadan Expressway we passed several accidents, but Pastor Shola said it was too dangerous to stop. There was no way of knowing whether it was a legitimate accident or a trick played by the area boys to lure motorists onto the side of the road where they'd be vulnerable to robbery.

The entrance to Redemption Camp was about thirty miles from Lagos and seemed more secure than the US consulate. A great crowd of people congregated outside of the gates: vendors selling mortars and pestles for making pounded yam, people waiting in line to show their credentials, and others begging for handouts from passing cars. Interspersed among them were armed guards in fatigues with patches on their shirts that read "Redemption Army." They waved in private cars and kept the pedicabs and *danfos* out.

As soon as we entered the gates I began to see why people talked about the church headquarters as the promised land. After a few weeks in Nigeria, I'd become accustomed to power outages and traffic snarls. But Redemption Camp had constant power, running water, manicured landscapes, even flush toilets. Once inside, one was shocked by the order and calm. Quaint street signs read "Holiness Road" and "Victory Avenue," and carefully painted houses were aligned in neat rows. At the corner was an enormous billboard advertising this month's Holy Ghost Service and its theme: "The Floodgates of Heaven." More signs pointed the way toward the post office or the university, and electric light posts bordered the roads. We passed a hospital, and Pastor Shola said that they had recently upgraded their maternity wing on account of all the babies that were born during the Holy Ghost Services.

When we made our way toward the outdoor amphitheater I found myself at a loss for words. Until that point the tent at Redemption Camp in Dallas had been the largest I'd ever seen. But here the outdoor amphitheater went on nearly as far as the eye could see—stretching so far into the distance that it had a computer-generated quality to it. It was an endless barnlike structure without walls, topped with a neat tin roof and solid wooden struts, punctuated every so often by bright electric lights, loudspeakers, and projection screens. Each section was labeled with a letter and number code to help people find their seats again if they'd gotten up to use the bathroom or answer an altar call.

Pastor Shola smiled at my shock. "Just wait," he said. We settled into a row of plastic chairs in row 5K, at least a quarter-mile away from the massive altar. Mrs. Shola brought out a mat for the children to lie down on later that night, and opened a picnic basket full of food that she'd toted from Ibadan along with a stack of porcelain plates and stainless-steel silverware. When she realized that I hadn't brought my own food she shrank the family's portions of goat and *jollof* rice, despite my protestations. We'd arrived a bit late, so we missed much of the opening worship service. The first preacher was in the middle of the sermon, which was translated simultaneously from English into Yorùbá by a translator who stood next to the preacher on the stage and copied his gestures.

Pastor Adeboye didn't come onto the stage until a few hours into the service, and when he did, he was wearing traditional Nigerian clothing, shimmering white fabric with red stripes, not the Western suit that he'd worn back in Floyd, Texas. His sermon centered on the idea of abundance, and the fact that all the world's abundance is controlled by God. He told the story of a young man who ran up to him after a sermon he gave in 1981. The young man prostrated himself, wordlessly stuffed something into the pastor's jacket, and then ran away. It was a fifty-pound note. Pastor Adeboye called the young man back, and the young man explained that he wanted to give something to God. The pastor prayed for him, asking God to return blessings to him for his faithfulness. When they met years later at another church event, the young man—now in his thirties—came up to Pastor Adeboye and said he now owned a school and a home of his own.

"The Lord is enough for our lack," Pastor Adeboye proclaimed, and the congregation melted into applause. He told the crowd that if we arrived with any form of sickness or disease, we'd go home healed—and if we gave freely to God, we could expect to get the money back a few weeks later, increased a thousandfold. Unless, of course, we were living in a state of sin. In that case we needed to run—not walk—to the altar and surrender our lives to the Lord.

Pastor Adeboye reminded us that God had a plan of coverage that included every man. God wanted hell to be empty. The whole purpose of the Holy Spirit was for missions, and we each had a mandate to invite as many people as possible to share in the blessings of God. That didn't necessarily mean to go out to the remote corners of the world to preach the gospel, but rather to stay where we were and preach through our professions. He reminded us that it wasn't the careful articulation of the message that would win souls to Christ, but rather the fact that the Holy Spirit was living in and working through us.

Between the preaching and the healing, right after thousands took communion, there was a moment when the horn players and drummers pushed the melody past the point of cerebral enjoyment, into a booming and trilling place where the heart soared away from the head. Sleepy men and women rose out of their seats and leapt into the air, lifting up their hands. Their voices glided into a space where language broke its leash from meaning. The atmosphere was so charged that my own heartbeat quickened. On the overhead projectors I watched grown men and women crying, their hands waving wildly in the air as they called out to Jesus to heal them. Pastor Adeboye's voice boomed from the speakers, but I couldn't quite understand it. He might have been speaking in Yorùbá, or maybe in tongues. The fleet of preachers who manned the altar had tossed their jackets off and pushed their shirtsleeves up, the better to move among the people who had come to the front for cleansing.

From the long line of people marching from the altar to the administrative center just left of the stage, it looked as if a thousand people had been saved. After they devoted their lives to the Lord and recited the salvation prayer in unison, the huge crowd of men, women, and children marched stage left. They followed a young usher who held a wooden sign with a long handle reading *Counseling*, who led them to a series of desks. Pastor Shola explained that church staff would review their stories and needs and collect their contact information in order to assign them to one of the churches within a five-minute walk in every town and city in southern Nigeria.

I knew that as soon as the newly saved repeated the words to the salvation prayer they'd feel all their petty anxieties melt away. But I also knew that by the time they walked

back to their seats and searched for handkerchiefs, their ec-
static feelings would have faded a bit. And by the time they
left the amphitheater, they'd probably be stuck in their heads
again. But when they went back to church on Sunday they'd
find a community. No one in their new congregation would
let them go hungry. Young men and young women would
meet and fall in love. With the church's help, people who
needed visas or medical procedures would have an easier
time navigating regulations and government agencies. Older
women would talk the young women through the trials of
marriage and child-rearing, and old men would sit together
outside the church and complain about the latest delay in receiving their pensions. No matter who was elected president
or which group of workers went on strike, the church would
support each other and help each other. They wouldn't be
alone anymore.

ᨆ

I stayed at Redemption Camp for two more days, sleeping
at a Western-style hotel in the middle of the compound
while Pastor Shola and his family headed back to Ibadan.
Thanks to my contacts back in Texas, I had near total access to pastors and staff, although I wasn't able to arrange
an interview with Pastor Adeboye. My liaison—a mid-level
pastor—promised that something could be worked out at
the convention.

I completed my interviews sooner than I expected and
walked around the compound for a while with a low-grade
headache. After several weeks of navigating Ibadan and Lagos, it was almost disconcerting how empty the streets were
here. People got around by car and the paramilitary troop-
ers kept the vendors and beggars out. Outside of the hotel,

when two small children came too close to a large, regal
wedding party, the Redemption Army officer shooed them
away fiercely with a baton. I abandoned my walk and went
back to my hotel room to type up notes from the interviews
I'd conducted. They had all started to sound the same. The
world presented some sort of painful obstacle—infertility,
abuse, poverty—and believers called out to God to hear their
prayers. God intervened, either by providing the very answer
that someone had in mind, or through more creative means.
A ready-made family in the shape of a marriage to a wid-
ower. A job. A ticket to America for a much-needed surgery.

I flipped through my notebooks. Interspersed between
the notes from interviews and sermons were all the little details about what I was seeing—the names of songs, whether
they were sung from old British hymnals, projected trans-
parencies, or more often by heart. Little observations about
what people were wearing or what kind of flowers adorned
the altar. No detail was too small. Littered within those ob-
jective accounts were my own reactions—commentaries on
the pastor's style, whether or not the people were engaged in
the message, where I was sitting.

I had learned to take notes from watching my mother
in church as a child. As soon as the pastor started speaking she'd thumb to a clean page in a cheap spiral notebook
and mark down the date at the right-hand edge of the page
and the title in the center. She wrote quickly, with a blue
Bic pen, capturing the pastor's sermon practically verbatim.
While my brothers doodled on the church bulletin, I sat
beside her with my own little notebook, writing down all
those rules for living in my childish cursive.

Now I saw how in a similar way I had tried to sum
up that entire trip to Nigeria in my steno pads, capturing

everything and leaving nothing to memory, so I could an-
alyze it later and finally get to the root of things. I'd set off
on that Airbus for Nigeria thinking I could sift through the
history of my childhood faith, weigh the truths and false-
hoods, and settle the question of my belief once and for all.
Either I'd find some pure core of truth and become devout
again, or I'd decide that it was all a lie and I'd become non-
chalant about my unbelief, like a man I met who proudly
hung a "Certificate of Debaptism" in his office. Either way
I'd stop being haunted by the question of faith. But as I sat
there in my luxurious hotel room in Redemption Camp, it
all felt like a ridiculous enterprise. There was nothing in
these notes that shed any light whatsoever on the question
of faith. I don't know what I thought I could find by recording every detail of those sermons and conversations and
interviews. It seemed nonsensical, like the people who tried
to weigh a body at the moment just before and after death
to prove that the soul existed. There was no point in using
the tools of the physical world to prove that the spiritual
world existed.

I remembered the story of Jennie Glassey, my favorite of
all the spirit-swept women from the nineteenth cenury that
I'd read about back in Houston. At seventeen Jennie left her
family in a pew at a camp meeting in Missouri and raced up
the aisle to claim her share of the kingdom. She repeated
the words to a black-bearded traveling preacher's salvation
prayer, and then she threw off her future as a farmer's wife
like a too-tight corset and pledged herself to the service of
God until the end of time. Jennie's family probably thought
her newfound faith would wind down to a slow, steady hum,
but days later God himself appeared at her bedside and told
her to spread his message in the mission fields of West Africa.

At first she resisted the Lord's call, saying that she was just a girl without means who couldn't speak any African languages. And then the Lord promised her that he would pave the way before her and grant her the ability to speak in strange tongues. Jennie obeyed, leaving her parents' farm and following the traveling preacher and his wife to St. Louis. Four days after her baptism, Jennie fell into a trance in which an angel presented her with a heavenly scroll, marked with strange characters she had never seen before. When the journalists came to interview her, she told them the angel first read the Book of Psalms and then the entire Bible aloud in a strange language that the reporters categorized as "African." She followed along in her Scottish brogue, riffing and rolling between tricky syllables until that tongue seemed as natural as English.

Later that summer, Jennie stood up in front of a raucous crowd at a faith-healing camp meeting and gave her testimony. After demonstrating the many languages the Lord had given her, she told of her plans to travel as a missionary to Africa. When someone asked how she would finance her trip, she tossed her auburn hair and replied that she didn't have any money, but she was confident that the promises of God were sufficient, and she would not starve.

Liverpool was only meant to be the first stop on Jennie Glassey's journey to Sierra Leone, but when she and her companions arrived in that sprawling port city, they ran out of money and were taken in by a sympathetic evangelist. For three long years they saved and scrounged, never giving up hope. Jennie wrote cheerful letters back to the States telling of new evidence of the Lord's faithfulness. She claimed to receive thirteen new teeth at the hand of the Lord, as well as more languages, and according to her friends she even acquired a sudden and mysterious talent for needlework and instrumental music. When a representative from a church mission group arrived in Liverpool to investigate her claims of miraculous languages, Jennie kept her mouth closed, perhaps sensing that he intended to unmask her. She wrote later that when the missionary instructed her to speak in tongues, she felt an unseen force surrounding her, compelling her to be silent.

Jennie Glassey kept her lamp filled until the end of her life, though the bridegroom tarried far longer than expected and she never made it to Africa. She and her fellow missionaries ended up in Palestine instead, but when they arrived, it turned out the Palestinian people couldn't understand a word they said. God, who could do all things, had given Jennie thirteen new languages with which to speak, but in the end it seemed that he had given her the wrong ones. Her companions headed back to America in shame, but Jennie spent another fourteen years as a missionary, roaming the deserts spreading the word of the Lord with the help of a native woman who served as her interpreter.

In that camp meeting in Missouri, Jennie claimed her place in the kingdom. Throughout all kinds of trials and tribulations she clung to God and kept that vision alive. Perhaps that's what it meant to be faithful. Jennie's belief was so strong and fierce that it carried her even when it seemed the God she worshipped had let her down. Maybe it wasn't actually God who had saved her, just like it might not have been God who saved all those people who lined up at the altar during the Holy Ghost Service a few days before. Perhaps it was their belief in God that gave them the strength they needed to save themselves.

❦ Chapter 15 ❦

The Virgin

Something about Yemi reminded me of my father back in his glory days, at his full height and strength. Both were tall and pleasing-looking, if not quite handsome, and both were mischievous and irreverent. They each had a kind of natural confidence that didn't come off as egoistical, maybe because it was paired with an easy charm and an endless curiosity about other people. Like my father, Yemi had a dim view of human nature. But where my father was infuriated by the way people constantly let him down, Yemi was delighted that people continually proved him right.

We'd first been connected by Gary Foxcroft, the aid worker from the documentary film. Yemi and his friends regularly traveled from Ibadan to Akwa Ibom to visit Sam Itauma's center, bringing them supplies and doing their best to draw international media attention to their case. Gary said that if I was serious about going out to see the children in Akwa Ibom, Yemi would be my best bet. He was the only person Gary would trust to get me there or to arrange security for the trip. Gary said it would be expensive to hire armed guards—at least ten thousand naira—but he insisted it was the only way for me to make the trip safely.

My first meeting with Yemi was at Spices, the campus bar at the University of Ibadan. There were only a few people there in the afternoon, and I was easy to spot. Yemi wore delicate wire-rimmed glasses that made him look somewhat like a Russian revolutionary. His hair was cropped close against his skull and a clump of keys dangled against his chest from a lanyard. We shook hands and then Yemi and I and his friend Jude drank from twenty-ounce bottles of Star beer and shared bowls of *ponmo*—roasted cow skin—while Yemi told me how he studied outcasts.

"*Omoita*. It means a child of the outside," Yemi said. "It's the word we use for motor park agents. It's a stigma word, it automatically ostracizes. The government doesn't take care of these people because they are *omoita*. They are seen as nothing—not educated, not deserving of education."

Yemi's friend Jude nodded and drank his beer, looking dour. "We have a bad culture here. I love my country. I would die for it, but it's a bad culture."

Yemi explained that he was no stranger to religion. As a kid, he had gone through a Christian phase, and then he'd briefly converted to Islam. "I've read the Bible," he said cheerfully. "My favorite books are Lamentations and Ecclesiastes, because they're about the absurdity of life."

Now Yemi identified as a humanist. He was drawn to humanism because it was utterly devoid of the supernatural.

"This God stuff—Christian, Muslim, whatever. It's bullshit."

Jude threw his head back and stuck out his tongue. "Stop being so bad!"

I asked Yemi if it was possible for atheists to thrive in Nigerian society.

"Oh yes, I think so," he said, his eyes dancing. "The language of money takes over. When you get money, nobody cares. People would just pray that the Lord would reveal himself to me."

After that first meeting we saw each other nearly every day. Yemi picked me up in his prized possession, a sleek late-model Honda Civic, and then drove fast through the streets, honking constantly at people he recognized. "How do you like my Nigerian ghetto?" he'd ask me, dodging dogs and vendors and potholes. As we drove we sketched out our lives for each other and before long we were getting past the surface and into the core of things. We talked about our ambitions and our dreams, our relationships. He teased me that as close as we were becoming, he knew Americans well enough. They buddied up to you quicker than anyone but when they left they were gone for good. He mimed picking up the phone and calling me a year from now, and I'd squint and say, "Yemi? Yemi who?" I shook my head furiously. That would never happen, I told him. We were in it for good.

Yemi's favorite topic was his beloved country, with its tangled history of wars and violence and colonialism. Nigeria was a mess, he said, shaking his head. In the fifty years since independence, the country had hardly had any credible elections. For almost a quarter of its history, Nigeria was led by a series of military dictators, each one fiercer than the last. In the late 1960s, the country entered the devastating Nigerian-Biafran War, which resulted in the death of millions of people. These days, Yemi explained, over half of Nigeria's population lived in dire poverty. Despite taking in annual proceeds of over $20 billion, largely from oil revenues, the government failed to provide basic services to its citizens, much less any kind of safety net for the poor, elderly, or mentally ill. The Christian south blamed the Muslim north for everything from poisoning vegetables to bombing churches to taking more than their share of power. The north blamed the south for taking the bulk of the oil profits from the Niger Delta. Yemi himself blamed a culture of widespread corruption, in which powerful politicians diverted millions of dollars of oil revenue to their own bank accounts while most people in the rural regions lived on less than a dollar a day. When they fell sick they had to pay before a doctor would even look at them, which was part of the reason why the life expectancy for the average Nigerian was barely fifty years. Yemi reminded me that when it came time for President Obama to visit Africa for the first time as president, he bypassed Nigeria and flew into Ghana instead. "I don't blame him a bit," Yemi said.

As we drove out of the main town, through the verdant green hills of Ibadan, Yemi explained that during the heady mid-seventies, when oil revenues tripled in the space of two years, trains crisscrossed the south and it was safe to travel. But when the oil bust hit a few years later, the bush crept over the train tracks again and no one dared drive at night. He pointed out the homes that had been abandoned half-built when oil prices started falling, and he said that was the same time that churches had started sprouting up like mushrooms. There was the Redeemed Church, which was seen as more middle class; Deeper Life, known for its emphasis on purity; the Mountain of Fire and Miracles, which claimed to heal people from HIV and AIDS; and countless others.

Yemi's own wife converted to Christianity in those years, and he wasn't sure that spirituality had much to do with her conversion. But he didn't blame her. He spoke kindly of religious people and saved his bitterness for the pastors. He said they were vultures preying on the poor, the ignorant, and the superstitious. As he talked I thought of a clipping that one of Yemi's friends had shown me a few days before. The headline read "N50,000 Tithe Technically Knocked Out 8 Years of Barrenness of the Womb." In the accompanying article, a man wrote of how he had received a half-million-naira contract and paid a tithe of 10 percent, and then, shortly after, his wife miraculously conceived a child after years of infertility. Similar signs were posted all throughout the city, advertising miracle services with slogans like "Expect the Unusual and Supernatural." Some encouraged couples trying to conceive to bring baby clothing or bottles, so the pastors could pray over those objects. One poster promised a special anointing for twins and triplets, quick marriage, easy baby delivery, and godly riches. Another promised deliverance from "marital delay, barrenness, poverty, failure, lack of tangible achievement, curses, and spiritual wreckage." Another featured a whole series of full-color photographs of people who stood on the stage holding a microphone, sharing their stories with the congregation. *HIV 1 and 2 healed,* the captions read. *Healed of heart enlargement. 17 years staphylococcus, five years piles cured. Salvation granted and ten years of barrenness broken.*

Yemi pointed out that as Nigerians converted to Pentecostal Christianity, there was an uptick in traditional beliefs as well. The more people believed in the Holy Ghost, the more they were inclined to believe in his enemies. That's what he said had happened in the Niger Delta state of Akwa Ibom. For centuries, witches had lurked at the fringes of society. Witch-hunting crusades were common as recently as the 1970s, when volunteer armies of fierce-eyed young men would go from village to village with machetes and sticks, forcing everyone into a central square. Their leaders would study the faces of the men and women and then subject those they suspected of witchcraft to age-old tests—burning them with hot metal, rubbing red pepper into their eyes, covering them with biting ants, and forcing them to eat the poisonous *esere* bean. But it wasn't until the twenty-first century, just after the release of the film that Helen Ukpabio made to teach her followers about the dangers of child witchcraft, that children in Akwa Ibom began to be accused. *End of the Wicked* followed the adventures of an eight-year-old girl whose soul is summoned from her sleeping body by a small witch-boy dressed in black. The two of them travel to an underground coven where a man in whiteface sits on a throne. The children are charged with draining money, health, and happiness out of their people, and for the rest of the film, they run amok, eating human flesh and causing their fathers to have heart attacks.

Helen's movie sold quickly in outdoor markets throughout the south, and the more popular the movie became, the more children there were in the street, running in packs and scavenging corncobs from the market. Every day there were new reports of child witches: a young girl in Ondo who was said to have changed into a cat and back again as her mother grew sicker and sicker; the two-year-old in Eket whose hunched back and small stature was a sure sign that the Devil was growing in him; or the six-year-old twins who were nearly buried alive by a man who believed they were behind the death of his wife. Helen had never met any of those particular children, but Yemi said that didn't mean she wasn't to blame.

Since that pair of Dutch filmmakers filmed their documentary, countless charity workers and reporters had bucked the travel bans to the Delta. Some of them had tracked down and interrogated Helen Ukpabio, and when they did, she denied the existence of any street children in Akwa Ibom, saying that the very notion of abandoning one's children was un-African. She claimed that, unlike other pastors, she didn't even charge fifty naira for delivering witches, and when she came across one, she didn't abuse them. She said she could deliver witches without even touching them, because the attack she made was a spiritual one. Once the possessed were delivered she sent them back to their families, where, according to her website, they lived happily ever after. It may look strange to Westerners when she prayed over child witches in that particularly ferocious way, but she would say that's because they are naïve and they don't know that the Devil sometimes takes the shape of a lamb. She even told a *New York Times* reporter that the children who had been filmed and photographed with wounds and scars from deliverance ceremonies were likely actors, and even if their wounds were real, there were many ways that children could be maimed.

Back at our usual spot at Spices, Yemi said that after all the negative attention she'd received from the international press, there was no way that Helen would consent to an interview with me. I told Yemi that I wanted to go to Akwa Ibom anyway and he shook his head, saying the Niger Delta was no-go these days—even the oil workers with their armored vans weren't leaving their compounds anymore. A trip like that would mean hiring armed guards to escort us to and from the airport, and even then the chances of a kidnapping were probably four in ten. As we ate and drank he told me story after story of kidnappings and shootings, but when he was done I counted out ten thousand naira and put the stack of bills on the table. He looked at the pile of money and leaned back with his arms folded and his mouth puckered.

"What's there for you?" he asked.

I picked at the label on my beer. My boyfriend, Jake, had asked me the same question when I told him I wanted to go to Akwa Ibom. Reporters had already covered the story—what would I see there that I couldn't read about in the *New York Times*? I couldn't really explain it. I tried to explain to Yemi that I had grown up believing the same thing as those pastors, thinking that there were evil spirits lurking around every corner. I could see how easy it would be for a pastor to make those children the scapegoat for everything that had gone wrong with the community, and I could imagine how hard it would be for anyone else in the congregation to defend them. I told Yemi that I'd come to Nigeria to take a good look at the church and make up my mind about it. The churches that I visited and the interviews I conducted showed me one side. But this was part of the legacy of Pentecostalism as well—a crucial part—and it wasn't unique to Nigeria. Surveys of Americans showed that a majority of us also believed that people could be possessed by demons. So I needed to face it. I needed to see the bad along with the good.

Yemi sighed. "I'll give you one day," he said. "One day, one night, then we get out."

In the week before the trip to the Delta I busied myself with more interviews and made several trips to the visa office in an effort to get my papers renewed. Mrs. Afolabi, the woman I'd met in the Atlanta airport, checked on me regularly, calling to make sure I had everything I needed and even stopping by the university to inspect my room and scold the mistress of the residence hall about the holes in my mosquito net. It was the least she could do, she said, pointing out how I'd helped her and her husband with their bags back in Atlanta.

When I finally made it out to visit them, the three of us toured their house slowly. Mrs. Afolabi pointed out the empty place in the kitchen that would soon hold the washing machine, opened her closet of Nigerian clothes for me to try on, and showed me the orange trees in the backyard, along with the herbs, some of which we could name and rename in English and Yorùbá.

We landed in a long indoor sun porch that ran across the full length of the front of the house. It was cooler there, and the electricity wasn't working that day. Outside a group of men worked under the hot sun, digging holes to install pipes for Mrs. Afolabi's new washing machine. Mrs. Afolabi served a plate of peeled oranges, Nigerian style—a special cut that removed the green skin and membrane from the oranges, leaving only the ripe orange fruit. Pastor Afolabi sat on one end of the porch in a house-shift, a dress-like garment Nigerian men sometimes wear while relaxing at home.

Mrs. Afolabi unwrapped her *gele*, an extravagant headdress, and fanned her shaved, graying hair. She disappeared and came back with a shoebox full of photographs. She lifted one after another from the shoebox and put them in my hands. We sat close as she narrated the stories behind each one. "This is my daughter's wedding," she said, passing me the next one. I tilted the photograph to make the thumbprints disappear and pronounced the wide-eyed girl and the delighted man "beautiful." A few minutes later Mrs. Afolabi presented another photo—smaller than the rest, sent from the United States, where her daughter's family now lived. It showed a bewildered boy of seven months. The Afolabis had four girls—all very successful, all but one happily wed. It was that last one who worried them a bit. She was in her forties now and it was starting to feel like she might go all of her life without knowing that special blessing God has for wives and mothers.

Pastor Afolabi asked how old I was, and they both started when I said I was thirty, protesting that I didn't look it. "The husband will come," Beatrice said firmly, and I smiled and said I hoped so too. I told them about Jake, thinking that it would put them at ease. The Afolabis seemed relieved to hear that he was well educated and held a good job, but Pastor Afolabi didn't seem to like the idea that he was a boyfriend and not a fiancé. He shook his head and said I should be careful about getting too close to someone without marrying him.

The afternoon was fading, the sun hitting the south wall, and we still had a stack of photographs to get through. Then Pastor Afolabi cleared his throat and leaned forward toward me. He said that there was something he wanted to ask me one day, when the time was right, but he didn't want to offend me. I smiled up at him and said that he could ask me anything he liked.

"I want to ask," he said with a slight tremor in his voice, "if you've been able to keep yourself pure with that boyfriend of yours."

I stuttered and blushed.

"I'm asking as a father," he assured me, "a pastor." He gestured to the large Bible that sat on the table beside his chair, so tattered that it appeared to be more a stack of papers than a bound book. At my side Mrs. Afolabi patted my hand supportively. I didn't blink. As a girl I had been taught that my body was a temple, to be guarded and kept pure until I left my father's house and devoted myself to my husband. I had been taught that it wasn't enough to merely believe in God. You had to keep yourself pure and free of sin or stain. You had to live out that belief through the process of sanctification. To become sanctified was to become holy. Any sin or stain was a break in the compact, and would keep you separated from God. You had to watch yourself continuously because the Devil was cunning and was always looking for a way to tempt and corrupt you. A sin wasn't just a lapse—it was a rebellion against God. The pastor knew that if I had sinned by allowing my body to be corrupted, by having sex outside of marriage—then I was vulnerable to the work of the Devil.

There was no way that I could hedge around the question or refuse to answer. The pastor told me he was asking as a pastor and a father. His eyes were kind—he must have seen it happen so many times before. A girl was weak and she opened her body to sin, stepping away from the protection of God. She left the blanket of protection and the Devil gained a foothold. That was what he wanted me to avoid. The door that, once opened, couldn't be unlocked again. I was young and full of promise, and it was essential that I be kept pure.

I imagined how it would go if I had been honest. The pastor's face would fall. He would be so sorry for me. If I admitted my sin, he would take my hand and pray with me, to ask the Lord for forgiveness. Our God was a stern God, but above all he was forgiving, and there was nothing that could not be redeemed.

But if I wasn't actually sorry for it, then that would mean I was truly lost. A subtle but unmistakable distance would grow between us. The pastor's face would curl up; he wouldn't leave it alone. He would try to understand, try to reason with me, and present biblical evidence that I was wrong. I would refuse to accept that evidence, and the conversation would disintegrate. I would make the long trip back to the university feeling shame in every part of my body.

But I didn't want to leave the circle. I wanted to stay here, on the warm sun porch, with these kind people, who looked at me fondly. Like a daughter. Who were pleased with me and delighted to have beliefs in common. And so I answered yes. I told the Afolabis that I had kept myself pure. But that meant slicing away the unacceptable part of myself, paring myself down so I fit into a belief system that would have otherwise scorned me. I watched Pastor Afolabi's face loosen, and he clasped my hand and brought it toward his chest. "Thank God!" he cried with real passion. I felt as distant from him as I had felt from my mother and father the day they told me how they'd read my journal. I trained my mouth to smile and waited a reasonable length of time before stretching and saying that I'd better get back to the university before dark.

A few days later, I agreed to join the Afolabis for their Sunday service at a small, one-room Baptist church in a rural part of Ibadan. Pastor Afolabi had led the church since the early eighties, the same year the Nigerian Baptist Convention had passed a policy statement that attempted to put a stop to rapidly spreading practices like jerking or weeping while praying, shouting "Hallelujah" or "Yes!" during prayers, laying hands on people to give them the Holy Spirit, or "speaking in tongues which nobody understands or can interpret." But most of the pastors simply ignored these new policies, as Pastor Afolabi had, or left the Baptist church for newer denominations like the Redeemed Church. Most of the Baptist churches in Nigeria now worshipped in the exuberant style that was once outlawed.

Pastor Afolabi had been retired for nearly a year and had passed the torch to a glowing young man, who on the day of my visit agreed to surrender a share of the stage so that Pastor Afolabi could introduce me to the congregation and tell them the story of our miraculous meeting in the Atlanta airport. I listened to this introduction not from the safety of my front-row seat, where I'd been tucked in next to Mrs. Afolabi, but rather from the middle of the stage, where Pastor Afolabi had strong-armed me a few minutes before. Pastor Afolabi was no longer wearing the red cable-knit sweater he'd been wearing at the airport or the beige house-shift he'd had on the last time I'd seen him. Now he was a Yorùbá king, with his purple robe billowing around him in yards and yards of sequined, jeweled fabric. He held the microphone and smiled at the congregation, clearly enjoying their favor and attention. Meanwhile I stood in front of him, peering out nervously at the packed room.

"We all know whites don't talk to each other—they don't even look at each other, much less us—but here was this white American girl, and she came out of nowhere to help us. It was an answer to prayer."

The new pastor sat behind him, wearing a dark suit and glossy dress shoes. He was smiling good-naturedly, and I thought it was kind of him to give Pastor Afolabi a few more minutes in the spotlight.

"Here's the other thing," Pastor Afolabi said, gearing up for another big revelation. "This girl, even though she has been in America all her life—even though she is almost thirty—she has kept herself pure for marriage. This girl is a virgin."

There was nothing I could do. Pastor Afolabi was on fire. The congregation was receiving it all with perfect attention. When he finished his speech, people sprung to their feet, clapping and stomping. My face burned. At Pastor Afolabi's prompting, the whole church stood as one body and prayed that the Lord would keep me safe in this strange country. They prayed that my boyfriend and I would find happiness and commit ourselves to one another and to God. They prayed for me to have traveling blessings on the dangerous roads here in Nigeria, as Pastor Afolabi had mentioned that I would be going to the Niger Delta next week. His announcement had been received with gasps of surprise.

When the congregation bowed their heads and raised their hands toward me, pleading with God for my safety as Pastor Afolabi led the communal prayer, I bent my head, willing myself to stop blushing, trying to receive the prayers the way they were meant, counting the seconds until I could

retreat from the stage. My eyes swept out across that congregation and I knew that any of those men and women who
were appealing to God on my behalf would happily take me
into their homes if I asked them to. They would treat me like
a sister, like a daughter, just as the Afolabis had. They saw
me as a fellow believer, and my supposed purity was proof
that we had a God in common. It didn't matter that I was
from a country six thousand miles away, on the other side of
the world. We didn't even need to share the same language.
Our shared faith was enough to make us family. If the congregation could have peeled off my outer shell and seen the
impure life that I led back home, their calls for my protection might have shifted into prayers for my repentance. But
as far as they knew, I was on their side—God's side—and so
they only wished to protect me from evil in any form.

Chapter 16

On the Far
Side of the Fire

When she was consecrated as an apostle of the Lord, Helen Ukpabio wore a dress made of shimmering blue and white fabric and a wide-brimmed white hat, and a troupe of Nollywood actors came all the way from Lagos to the Niger Delta to honor her. The white and silver checkered pattern on her dress glowed and refracted the light from the many cameras in the room. She knelt on the marble altar and twenty men surrounded her, some in black clerical robes and some in colorful dashikis. They held their palms out to her as if to give her a portion of their spiritual power.

Years after the ceremony took place, I watched on video as Helen swayed in syncopation with the bishop's voice as he called out to God in roiling tones, calling God's spirit down upon her. He blessed her as a woman of God and wrangled to get a place for her in the kingdom. The whole room prayed with him in the language the original apostles had gotten straight from heaven after Jesus died on the cross—the language that knows no earthly translation, the language of the Spirit. After a while Helen blotted her face with a handkerchief. Toward the front of the sanctuary, rows of women in white dresses and shiny gold headdresses prayed with one eye open, so they could be ready to burst into song when the praying was done.

On the marble altar, between Helen and the bishop, sat a gold brocaded chair. The bishop pointed for her to sit, and then the camera cut out for a moment. When the filming resumed, Helen was sitting on the chair, her face stretched toward the sky, with an expression of utter calm and peace. The bishop didn't need the microphone anymore; his voice had taken on that Pentecostal rhythm and roll. He held the back of Helen's head with one hand and jabbed the other toward her face, stopping just short of making contact. A group of men gathered around her now, holding their hands toward her, praying loudly. Just in front of the camera stood a group of younger men. They held their cell phones out to capture the moment. Helen's hands were behind her back and her face was tilted slightly to the right. Her face looked soft and unlined and calm. Her lips were the same color as the rest of her face. She wore no make-up and her hair was gathered back underneath her hat in a plain style. Her modest pumps lay next to her in a pile.

In the years since that ceremony was filmed, Akwa Ibom had changed. Not so long ago the women there grew yams and maize in patches of cleared bush, but now the only thing that took root was elephant grass, razor-sharp and inedible. The okra and palm trees were slow to flower, and every year the cassava grew smaller. The men had pawned their outboard motors and left their skiffs to rot on the riverbanks; they said the fish that used to nest in the mangrove roots had fled deep into the sea. Whatever sickness afflicted the land seemed to be spreading to the people. Women's wombs closed up too early and when children were born they were often listless and small. Their bellies grew faster than the rest of them and some of them couldn't take a breath without choking.

The European aid workers blamed the ExxonMobil installation on the eastern side of the Qua Iboe river. They pulled well-worn maps from their messenger bags and outlined the slow creep of crude oil into the rivers and tributaries, the equivalent of an Exxon *Valdez* spill every year for forty years straight. The more adventurous among them snuck out of their heavily guarded hotel compounds to take blurry cell phone shots of the gas flares spitting fire into the night sky. Back in the safety of the hotel they poured tall glasses of duty-free scotch and sat by the pool telling stories until their pale faces turned red with indignation. They talked of what Shell did to Ken Saro-Wiwa, the travesty of Nigeria's missing $22 billion in oil revenue, the spiraling poverty in the Niger Delta, and the millions of naira the governor had been handing over to Nollywood stars. In the last hours before dawn the aid workers started slurring their words and widening the circle of blame to Nigeria's colonial legacy and their own countries' demand for fossil fuels. When they slept they tossed and turned alone in king-size beds as the rain pounded down onto the hotel's tin roof.

But Helen Ukpabio would say these aid workers were wrong. She'd scoff at the belief that strongly worded op-eds and environmental regulations could put the world right again. She'd say that the people of Akwa Ibom were not being ravaged from without, by impersonal demons of political corruption, environmental devastation, and disease, but rather from within, by sin and demonic attacks. The problem here was not material, she'd say, but rather spiritual. The people of Akwa Ibom didn't need better laws, or even food aid. They needed spiritual guidance about how to fight evil, and that's what her ministry offered.

There were some who believed that Helen was evil incarnate, who blamed her for the phenomenon of child-witchcraft accusations. They believed that if you removed pastors like her from the picture, families would remain whole and children would thrive. And there were others who would testify that Helen was a walking saint who had saved thousands. It was clear to me that, as with everything else, what you thought about Helen depended largely on where you sat.

॥

Early one Friday morning, Yemi and I took a flight from Lagos to Uyo, the capital of Akwa Ibom state. On the hour-long drive from the tiny airport to Sam Itauma's center, I sat between two off-duty policemen with AK-47s in the back of a rusty Nissan hatchback. The heat in the Niger Delta was overwhelming; the car had no air-conditioning and Yemi had instructed me to wear a long skirt, long sleeves, a scarf wrapped around my neck and a hat, in hopes that I might be mistaken at first glance for an albino. The policeman on my left couldn't have been more than eighteen, though he acted far older, solemnly combing the roadside for threats and frowning when his colleague laughed and joked with the driver. His partner knew a bit of English, and his eyes lit up when I told him I was from the US. "Obama's country!" he said excitedly, again and again, until Yemi rolled his eyes and shushed him.

Early in the trip we noticed crowds of men planting young palm trees along the road, weeding the median strips, and repainting white lines on the road at a furious pace. One of the policemen explained to Yemi in pidgin that the president was coming to Akwa Ibom tomorrow and the governor had ordered a major cleanup initiative in preparation. Yemi was delighted to hear the news and told me my chances of being kidnapped had just gone down significantly. Not only would there be extra security on the roads for the next several days, but odds were that any and all would-be kidnappers would be too busy making a few hundred naira as part of the governor's impromptu cleanup brigade.

The roads grew more ragged as we drove and there were fewer and fewer buildings of any kind. Parrots and cicadas squawked and buzzed through lush walls of green, and dark streams ran beside the gum trees that shaded the footpaths on the side of the road. At intersections, hawkers gathered around the car selling cellophane bags of "pure water" and roasted corn for twenty naira apiece. Under the gum trees on the roadside old men dozed and young women braided one another's hair. In the distance, we could make out the pipes and smokestacks from the ExxonMobil plant that loomed over the town, and smoke from the gas flares could just be seen over the dark line of oil palms at the edge of the horizon. We must have passed forty churches between Uyo and Eket: House of Favor, Tabernacle of Truth Ministries, Faith Builders Mission, Sanctified Apostolic, Holy Ghost Family Deliverance Ministries. I wrote the names of the churches down in a little notebook that I kept in my pocket, and every time I looked up from writing one name I'd look up and see another one. Yemi said it was that last church that was one of the worst offenders, but when I asked what they had done he just pursed his lips and looked away.

In Eket, we pulled onto a narrow dirt road marked by a makeshift sign reading "Child Rights and Rehabilitation Center." Yemi rolled down the window at last and craned his neck out, pointing and shouting. There was Sam Itauma's house, there was the clinic where they treated the children for parasites and malaria, there was the path to the outdoor kitchen where the children ate their meals. I pulled my scarf off and sat up straight, afraid of what I would see when we rounded the corner. The policemen seemed uneasy as well.

"There!" said Yemi, directing the driver to a dirt field ringed by a set of ramshackle concrete buildings in faded pastel colors. There were bits of colorful cloth all around the perimeter, and as we got closer I realized it was the children's laundry, drying on clumps of grass in the field. In the middle of the field, playing soccer barefoot, were the children I had come to see. We parked the car and when Yemi bounded out, the children stopped their soccer game and rushed toward him, whooping and hugging his legs and patting his pockets for gum. Their heads were shaved, boys and girls alike. While their arms and legs were thin, they all seemed whole. You had to look closely to see the scars.

A little boy tugged me away from the car, calling me *Miss* and watching me carefully to make sure I avoided the puddles. He led me toward Sam Itauma, who I'd recognized from the New York movie premiere despite the fact that he'd traded his suit for jeans and a baseball cap. Sam and Yemi exchanged a complicated handshake and Sam shook my hand formally at first, then pulled me in for a hug. He was very glad I came, he said. The more Westerners who visited, the more attention the politicians paid to the children. Sam explained that they had recently succeeded in getting a national child rights bill passed, but enforcement was always an issue. The policemen who were supposed to protect the children were just as afraid of them as the rest of the villagers. Sam said that recently a policeman in Eket had brought his own daughter to the center after he became convinced she was a witch.

A tiny girl of seven clung to Sam's arm as he spoke to us, and Sam explained that he had found her that morning, sleeping in a pile of cast-off clothing on the side of the road. She was so frail that at first he had thought that she was dead, but once she ate a Scotch egg he bought from a roadside vendor, she came into herself enough to tell him her story. Her name was Nkoyo and her grandfather said she was a witch, so her father beat her and kicked her out of the house. That had been over three weeks ago, and she had been sleeping on the street ever since. Nkoyo was bone-thin and her big belly poked out of a ragged, dark-blue Victorian-style dress. Her arms and legs were speckled with burns and other scars, and an ugly knot rose out of the back of her left hand. In her other hand she gripped a plastic toy alligator she had found in Sam's pickup truck, and over the course of an hour, she moved from Sam's arm into the midst of a group of children who seemed far more interested in her alligator than they were in her. Before too long, an older girl had her by the elbow and took her around the center: the crumbling cement-block boys' quarters, the UNICEF-funded girls' quarters, the school rooms, an open-air kitchen, an administrative center, and the field in the center of the compound. Later, Nkoyo would go to the clinic to be treated for worms and lice. Her wounds would be examined, and she'd see a social worker who would listen to her story and log the name of her accuser in a ledger. The next day she'd be paired up with an older girl who would be responsible for making sure she was getting along well with the others and eating and sleeping enough.

Beyond that, Nkoyo's future was uncertain. There were few jobs in Nigeria, though the children in Sam's center had big dreams. When I interviewed a few children in the one-room schoolhouse, one little girl lifted her leg onto the table between us to show me the scars from rope burns on her ankles before telling me she wanted to be an actress. She relayed her story in a matter-of-fact manner, taking great pleasure in signing her name in my notebook once the conversation was finished. She was the one who told me how the pastor brought her in front of the church and accused her of going to the witchcraft world while she was sleeping. He accused her of taking her mother's stomach, eating the baby that was growing there, and putting blood and water in its place.

As the shadows lengthened, the children on laundry duty gathered up the clothes that had been drying in the soccer field. Yemi, Sam, and I walked them through a thicket of yucca and cassava plants to an outdoor kitchen where village women were ladling scoops of rice and beans into tin cups. The children ate with their hands, perched on wooden benches while the cooks eyed them, shouting at them in Ibibio when they became too noisy. As we watched them, Sam told me he'd had a hard time finding kitchen staff when he first opened the center, despite the fact that jobs in Akwa Ibom were hard to come by. The women he approached had been afraid that they'd catch some spiritual contaminant at the center. But Sam was handsome and persuasive, and after a few weeks without any unusual sicknesses in their families, most of the women he'd hired lost their fears of the children and even started touching them occasionally, swatting their bottoms when they failed to queue up or patting their heads as they distributed food.

When the children finished their meals, I treated Sam and some of his staff to dinner at a restaurant in town. Over pounded yam and fish pepper soup, he told me how, just after Helen's film was released, he had come upon four children being attacked by a group of men and women carrying sticks and rocks and machetes. The mob believed the children were witches who had come to "bring down" the products in a nearby outdoor market. Sam convinced the mob to let him take the children into his home, and when word got out, children arrived on his doorstep at a rate of five or six per month, and he could never bear to turn any of them away. He approached the government to see if they could help, but the officials in charge of Akwa Ibom's hospitals and orphanages were worried that the children would spread the seeds of witchcraft to their wards. It wasn't until Gary Foxcroft became involved that Sam could finally get enough funding to turn his ramshackle collection of outbuildings into a formal charity operation that would eventually house nearly two hundred kids.

Sam and his staff did everything they could to give the children a normal life. Early on, they took them to soccer games in town to give them a chance to mingle with the rest of the community. "Then these men approached us at the stadium and said we had to leave before nightfall," Sam said, shaking his head. "They believed that was when the children would turn into witches. We did not budge in spite of the warning—it was a public place—and they turned into a mob and said they would stop us from ever going there again.

They said if we took the children into town they would use a bullet on us. So we left and haven't gone back."

At dinner I sat across from Ruth, a middle-aged graduate student in sociology who wore her long hair tightly bound into braids. She was writing her thesis on witchcraft accusations, and told me that she had become involved with Sam's center after she had brought food to a boy living in the street, only to have him run away in fear, thinking she had been trying to poison him. She and her husband were fairly well-off, and when her own children first asked her about the street children they passed on the roadside, she wasn't sure how to explain what had happened to them.

She decided to tell them the street children were God's children, but that just confused her own children even more. "If they're God's children, then why doesn't God take care of them?" they asked her. "Why doesn't he build them a house?" She laughed as she told me that—the things that children say. But I was quiet. They sounded like good questions to me, the kind of questions I probably should have been asking when I was a child.

∿

At twilight on Friday nights in Akwa Ibom, when people walked miles to the deliverance houses, the color that bloomed out of that green and brown world was nothing short of astonishing. There was magenta and gold-vermilion and cerulean blue and lavender. Families wore the same fabrics to show they were one people, and the women wore head wraps of the same material, wrapping the fabric around their heads like enormous, winding crowns. They walked like queens, backs ramrod straight, scolding the children as they chased one another along the paths. You could only tell they were poor because they had no shoes.

The deliverance houses were the shabbiest of all the churches, made of cast-off wood with rough concrete floors and repurposed tin roofs. They weren't tied to any larger church bodies, not the Redeemed Church or Christ Apostolic or even Helen's own denomination—Liberty Foundation Gospel Ministries. There were no artificial flowers on the altar in the deliverance houses, no polished cedar crosses, no hymnals or even Bibles. Sometimes there weren't even walls or floors, just hard-packed dirt with a few grimy plastic chairs. There were often leaks in the tall tin ceilings. Around here, roofs only lasted a couple of years because the acid rain from the gas flares ate away at the tin. During the day you could hear the water dripping into the buckets the pastor's wife put out to catch the water, but at night the sound of worshipping drowned it out.

First there were the praise songs, set to the beat by drums and tambourines and the women's soprano lilts. And then at an almost indecipherable moment some spirit burst through the crowd, creating a frenzy. Women clutched their chests and wept, men clapped their hands and pounced in place, pumping their fists and shouting as if boxing with a very large spiritual beast. The children let loose with their heavenly languages and cried out to Jesus. It was then that there was supposed to be healing and renewal and revelation, but instead something else happened. The pastor stood in front of his congregation and saw the women holding sick babies in their arms, their dark eyes asking him why. Maybe that was when he combed through the crowd and his eyes landed on one of the stubborn children, squirming in the back of the church. He remembered a film he saw once and curled a strong finger to draw that child up to the altar. When he did he came alive again, with the force of God behind him. His tongue loosened and he began preaching the way he was always meant to preach, because now it was clear that the sickness of this whole community was in this mischievous child. That child was the force behind his aunt's barrenness, his youngest sister's coughing fits, even the village's shrunken crops. The child protested but was not to be believed. After days of fasting, chained to the side of that deliverance house, he'd end up confessing his crimes. He'd be driven away, and then the village would finally have some peace again.

❦

Dinner ended early because Yemi insisted on dropping me off at the only hotel in town before night fell. He said the roads weren't safe for whites at night. The Belajno was right next to the ExxonMobil compound, but I saw no sign of the oil workers or any other guests. There was nothing to do in the hotel but type up my notes and read the testimonies of the children I had interviewed. Their stories were all very much the same.

My uncle's wife said I was a witch, that I was the one who wanted to kill and torture their children. She tied me with a rope. I did not think I was a witch.

My mother saw me sleeping different. She took me to the church for a long time. The church made me dry-fast with no water. Even when they gave me a bath they would put a cloth on my face so I couldn't drink. When I saw the wife of a pastor eating a cucumber I took it and ran away. The pastor ran after me and slapped me and tied my hands and arms and beat me with three brooms until 6:00. Then he called my grandfather. He said if I stayed in the house I would destroy everything. I was rooming on the street until they directed me here.

I greeted the pastor in our house. He called to me and said, Are you a witch? I said no. He beat me and dug a hole. He says if I don't say it he will bury me alive. So I said yes, I am a witch.

I lay on my king-size bed for a long time, thinking it through. I had spent the day at Sam's center, interviewing staff and taking the children's testimonies, and I still knew no more than when I started. There was nothing special about these children. Each one was just as beautiful and brilliant as any other child in the world. I was chasing clarity and understanding, thinking that if I only accumulated enough knowledge and evidence, I'd be able to wrap my mind around the phenomenon of child witchcraft accusations. I'd be able to find the people who were to blame and figure out the root cause of the evil they did, the true villain—whether it was Christianity or poverty, the multinational oil corporations or a government so corrupt that it wasn't able to help the children. It was the same impulse that had led me to interview Christians and transcribe sermons, to trace the roots of Pentecostal Christianity back to the Yorùbá tradition that I believed to be their original source. I thought that if I dug deep enough and went back far enough, the well would run clear.

I suppose I came by that compulsion honestly. The scholar Eileen Scully once described fundamentalist faith as "an anxious search for inviolate truth." I couldn't shake the feeling that there was a capital-T truth behind everything, and if I could only find it, then I would know what to do. But I'd been wrong every time. The more I dug into the history, the more I filled my notebooks with quotes from my interviews, the more contradictions and questions I came across, and the more doubt grew in my mind. The faith that did so much good for the people of Nigeria seemed to be behind so many wrongs as well. The very pastors who greeted me so warmly after church services were the same ones who were spreading the idea that people could be possessed by witches. There didn't seem any way that I'd be able to follow all the tangled threads within the history of the church and find some pure kernel of good or evil underneath it all.

For some reason I thought back to the time when I was eighteen and about to leave home for college. My father sat me down on a wicker loveseat on the porch and told me that the world was vast and beautiful and would never stop astonishing me. I should see as much of it as I possibly could. And then he said something I didn't understand. He told me I was young and I hadn't known true suffering yet. But he had, and it taught him that sometimes the world throws us so much pain that we may be driven to do things we never imagined, because we just can't see any other way. He then told a long story about a woman he met once who had been abused as a child and then became a drug addict and sold her body. "Can any of us really blame her?" he asked me. "After all she had been through?" Then he stopped talking, just sipped his Budweiser and looked out over the tobacco farm that lay beyond the porch. Deer fed on the corn that our landlord threw on the fields, and a lone red-tailed hawk played sentry from the top of a dead oak.

At the time I wondered about that woman, who she might have been, and how my father might have known her. I couldn't make much sense of my father's send-off. But now I think he was trying to tell me that life wasn't as black and white as Pastor Jim made it out to be, that not all sins necessarily had the Devil behind them. That life was messy, and it wasn't always possible to be pure. At that time, I had lived most of my life feeling safe and loved, but my father had grown up without those same protections I had. As a result, he spent his life trying to gain dominion over the anger and rage that lay deep inside of him. He didn't always succeed. Now I think he was telling me not to judge him too harshly for some of the things he had done. I think he hoped I would never know that same darkness myself, but in the meantime I should remember that as long as I went untried and untested, I didn't yet know what the darkness could do to me.

Chapter 17

The Edge of the Abyss

Wole Soyinka once wrote that the fundamental quality of Yorùbá existence is the awareness that there is an abyss running between the living and the dead. It was the job of the *babalawos* to perform spiritual maintenance so that everyone on the side of the living would be safe. They placated the dead and kept them from sending spirits to snatch the living into the seething cauldron of the great abyss. The *babalawos* walked the lines between life and death, and only in the dark times did the rest of us—the unholy ones—get closer than we should to that abyss. The rest of our lives were filled with daily concerns, but every once in a while, the caul was ripped off and we saw that other side for what it truly was. And only then did we learn who we were and what we believed in. That was my experience during my last few weeks in Nigeria.

I planned to go back to Redemption Camp to join over a million worshippers at the yearly convention. It would be the culmination of all my research. For the past few weeks I had been working with the church administration to finalize the visit, which would include a rigorous schedule of interviews with pastors, church members, and church leaders, including Pastor Adeboye himself. I imagined myself in a long, modest skirt and a sun hat, interviewing people and taking notes, photographing the buildings so that I could describe the details later. And then there was the service. I felt a thrill whenever I thought about it. How could I not be moved, standing in the midst of so many true believers?

A few days before I was supposed to leave for Lagos for the convention, Yemi suggested that we celebrate my time in Nigeria with a kind of farewell trip to the Erin-Ijesha waterfalls. If Yemi hadn't offered to make the drive in his Honda Civic, it was doubtful that we would have been able to go. Hired drivers wouldn't have wanted to risk getting stuck in the mud in the long unpaved roads that led to the waterfalls, and even if we could find one that did, the two-hour drive from Ibadan would be extremely expensive. But Yemi offered up his car, and we invited a few other friends: his coworker Tunde, a quiet man in his thirties who worked full time to pay for the education of his five younger siblings; a British historian named Henry; a French student called Gabriel; and Efi, a wide-eyed undergraduate at the University of Ibadan who had become a good friend of mine.

We set off for the waterfalls at six in the morning. I packed a duffel bag with snacks and towels, and we stopped a few times for roasted corn and *moin-moin*, the bean cakes sold on roadsides all around Nigeria. Yemi played Nigerian rap as we drove, and we all got on swimmingly, despite the fact that four of us were squished into the back of Yemi's car. Yemi teased me about skipping church. This particular Sunday was the first one in two months when I hadn't wrapped a scarf around my hair and settled into a plastic chair with my Bible in one hand and notebook in the other.

When we finally arrived, some of us took more convincing than others to strip down to our underwear and dive into the frigid pool beneath the falls, but eventually everyone was sopping wet. Tunde and Gabriel—the most adventurous—climbed deep inside the waterfall and dove the five or six feet into the pool. Efi snapped photos of us hamming it up, while Henry arranged us carefully for group portraits at the overlooks. I took pictures when no one was looking and caught Yemi belly-laughing when Tunde slipped on a rock and took an unintended dive. Toward the middle of the afternoon we bought cans of beer and old Sprite bottles filled with homemade palm wine, milk-white and frothy. I felt like a teenager again, and I could tell that everyone else felt the same way. I'd never heard Yemi or Gabriel laugh so much, or seen Efi so happy. For a day they were free of all the petty annoyances of life—power outages, the "go-slows" that made it impossible to make it from one side of Ibadan to another, the strikes that shut down the university several times a month. Instead we just reveled in being together.

As Efi and I stripped our wet clothes off behind large rocks and the boys packed up the car, two musicians came out of nowhere and played the talking drums for us to wish us well on our journey home. We gave them a few naira and set off south for Ibadan.

We had been driving for about an hour when it happened. A mist of light rain had obscured the road, or perhaps Tunde, who was driving, had drunk too much palm wine. I doubted it was the car—Yemi was fiercely proud of it and took it for maintenance regularly. Perhaps the potholes were to blame. Minutes before, we had been travelling far too fast and darting back and forth between the parts of the road that were worn away. I noticed Henry and Gabriel clinging to the handles of the car, giving me a nervous look. But none of us said anything. We didn't want to cast a pall on the trip by urging caution.

And then, before any of us could respond, we felt it. Tunde swerved suddenly, perhaps to avoid a pothole. He overcorrected, and I felt us losing control. Suddenly we were at the mercy of the car itself—a sleek, emerald-green thing that seemed bent on leaving the road. We picked up speed and careened in a tight circle, then hurtled into a thicket in the median of the highway.

I always thought that when I came close to death I would have some moment of clarity, or perhaps a moment of utter chaos and confusion. Everything that I loved most about the world would dart through my mind and I'd whisper some sort of final benediction over everything I was leaving behind. Maybe I'd even call out to God and beg for forgiveness for the last time. But instead I thought nothing at all. In that split second when I felt the car leave the road and tumble into the thicket—turning over at least twice—I simply held on to Efi as tightly as I could. There was only darkness when I closed my eyes.

Time thinned and stretched out. I waited for unconsciousness to hit, or the feeling of steel piercing my skin. But it didn't happen. I heard the sound of metal screeching on metal, and then there was stillness. I opened my eyes to the brightest world I had ever seen. My pink-and-blue sundress glowed in a thicket of green. Vines filled the car, having poured in when the windows broke when we flipped over. I brushed them aside and patted my skin, which seemed to have held together. Efi was on my lap, and she seemed whole as well, as did Gabriel and Henry beside me. Somehow the car had turned over and landed upright. We blinked and blinked, trying to get our vision back. I looked in front of me and saw red. The hood of the car had caved in and pinned Tunde's head down into an unnatural position. Bright-red blood trickled from the place where the car met his skull, and I yelled, pushing aside vines in an attempt to get to him. Towels and wet clothes and bags of *moin-moin* were everywhere, covered in thick dust from the impact.

What happened next happened in fragments. It seemed essential to get Tunde out of the car. In the US we would have left that task to the paramedics, but here they might not be coming, and who knew if the car would blow up. Yemi poured a bottle of water over my face, and when I wiped it off with my dress, I was shocked to see the same red blood that covered Tunde all over my dress. At the time I thought it was his blood, but later I'd catch a glimpse of myself in the mirror, and learn that the left side of my face had been slashed open, by glass or vines, and the skin around my other eye was bruising rapidly.

Henry went to the side of the road and tried to wave down passing vehicles. Twenty cars must have passed, but no one stopped. I remembered what Pastor Shola has told me about how people sometimes staged accidents with the intent of robbing would-be Good Samaritans. Finally an *okada* driver pulled over, keeping his distance while he eyed our wounds. Once he was satisfied the blood was real he called an ambulance on his cell phone. When it came, the driver seemed more concerned about getting us loaded into the ambulance quickly than tending to our injuries.

By that point Tunde had woken up. He kept rubbing his neck. Efi pressed a purple scarf against the wound on his head. The ambulance drove to Ife, a small city twenty minutes away where I had traveled just a week before to interview an eminent professor of Pentecostalism. In Ife, the ambulance driver pulled up in front of Adventist General Hospital and waved us past the waiting crowds of people outside of the hospital. When the nurses and doctors saw us, their hands leapt to their mouths. "Sorry-o," they said in pidgin, shaking their heads.

I lay on my back on an examining table and felt light-headed. The doctor began washing my face and using tweezers to remove glass and gravel and dirt from the vines. I cried out. Next to me, not even separated by a curtain, was a young man in his twenties whose finger had been mashed up, pulverized. He was quiet, but when I glanced over to him, I saw that his face was covered with tears.

The doctor who saw to my wounds soothed me. He told me that it was okay to cry as I was being stitched up. As a "white," my skin was more sensitive than the average Nigerian's skin, and so he made repeated trips to the hospital pharmacy for more painkillers. This made me even more upset. I left the hospital blood-splattered and in tears, the left side of my face bandaged and the right blackened. Tunde had to stay overnight for observation, though the doctors seemed confident that he'd recover with no permanent injuries.

Getting back to Ibadan was a blur. Yemi called a friend of his to come pick us up, but somehow he got into an accident on the way as well, and we ended up taking a cab back to Ibadan. I managed to sneak past the curious porters with my head covered. Fortunately, I had a bit of water left in my bucket from doing laundry the day before. I heated it with my kerosene stove and crouched in the shower, pouring the small portion of water over my hair, which was matted and caked in blood. When I poured the water over my head gingerly, clumps of hair came out and clogged the drain. As soon as I saw that hair my hands started shaking. It took me nearly a minute to realize that the doctor had shaved part of my head while putting in the stitches. That night I rolled up in my sleeping bag in the dark and felt something scraping at my neck. It was a shard of glass from the car windshield.

I called my mother the next morning and told the story in bits, so as not to upset her. She told me breathlessly that the day before, just as the accident happened, she felt so overcome with worry for me that she pulled over on a busy highway and prayed to God to keep me safe.

I spent my final week in Ibadan holed up in the tiny screened-in porch in my dormitory room, chain-smoking imported British cigarettes and reading a bad translation of *War and Peace* on my Kindle while the geckos darted across the screen of my window, their pale-colored undersides catching the glow from the screen. The trip to Redemption Camp—the lynchpin of all my research—was now impossible. The doctors at the clinic on campus insisted that I stay nearby so that the cuts behind my ear could be washed and bandaged daily. I was terrified of an infection, so I obeyed their orders.

Besides, all the adventure had been knocked out of me. I only wanted to be still and alone. When my hallmates walked by outside the window, I drew my cigarette down in my lap so they couldn't see its light. Before I left my room to make some rice on the kerosene stove, I listened at the door to make sure no one was around. I didn't want to answer any more questions about the accident or dodge inquiries about who was driving and who was to blame. When I did go out, strangers stopped me on the street, aghast at my cuts and bruises, and clutched their chests in sympathy.

Periodically people would come to see me, and most tried to put the accident in perspective. The vast majority said that God had protected me. His favor was what had kept me from slipping over the abyss. They told me to be thankful, to praise God for saving my life. I must have great work to do, they reassured me. A small percentage of my visitors—those who had already been suspicious of my habits of taking *okadas* and *danfos*—suggested that I had gotten what was coming to me. "This isn't like America," they warned me. "You have to be careful here."

Yemi stopped by once and winced at the sight of my bloodied bandages. His eyes darted around the room and he said it was good I was keeping a low profile. I didn't say much. I knew he was nervous. If word got out to his thesis committee about the accident it could have a major impact on his standing. He told me he was trying to raise the money to repair his car, cobbling together the small stipend he received for teaching and some money he'd received from a Norwegian woman he'd met at a humanist conference who ended up taking him under her wing. I felt sick when I thought about how much he loved the car and how hard it would be to replace it, and I knew he must be wondering why I didn't offer up a contribution, but I had spent the last of my grant funds pitching in for Tunde's medical bills, and if I gave more I wouldn't be able to pay my rent back home.

The differences between us swelled up in those final few moments together. I was going back to the US, to a country with a stable government, free public education, and hospitals that wouldn't turn you away if you came in bleeding and couldn't pay your bill. Yemi was staying here, continuing his role as a rabble-rouser, doing what he could to protect children like Nkoyo, protesting human rights abuses wherever he found them. We'd probably trade emails for a few months and like each other's photographs on social media, but after a while Yemi's prophecy would likely come true. The man who had been such a friend to me would fade away in my mind, until I could no longer call up the distinct contours of his face or the sound of his voice. I was always leaving behind the people I loved. When we hugged goodbye, I had trouble meeting his eyes.

Later that night, when my eyes were exhausted from reading, I washed the raw area behind my ear, and then I lay on top of my sticky sleeping bag on the narrow pallet of a mattress, holding my knees to my chest. There was nothing left to do. It was just me and the lizards darting across the screen on my porch, lit up by candlelight. That night I was afraid and I didn't know why. My brain buzzed and my heart beat too fast. The air was thick and humid and the forest beside the dormitory was croaking and lurching. If I searched through the sounds I could hear the lions roar in the university zoo a few blocks away.

A few weeks before, an undergraduate at the University of Ibadan had told me a story, one that I had never been able to prove. He told me how, twenty years ago, an earnest young Christian slipped into the zoo late at night with some of his friends and together they pried open the heavy iron bar in front of the lion's cage. As the lion slunk around in the shadows on the other side of the cage the student rebuked it loudly in Jesus's name. He must have imagined himself to be Daniel in the lion's den, and thought that God would pacify the beast and keep him safe because of his faith. The student stood tall, holding that door open, shouting and cursing, remembering the verses in the Bible where Jesus told us that we could do anything—move mountains, even, if only we believed. The lion paced faster and faster, confused and alarmed to have his silence disturbed. And then, as the boy's friends watched, the lion charged. Early the following morning the zookeepers brought his body out in pieces.

Hannah, the German lecturer, had been in the room with Efi and me while the undergraduate was telling the story. She'd choked on a spoonful of *jollof* rice and her eyes had flashed. Pure idiocy, Hannah had said, shaking her head. But Efi was quiet. She went to church every Sunday— to one of the student fellowships that met in the open-air worship park on the south side of campus, and I could guess what she was thinking. That boy didn't believe enough, or he wasn't pure enough. Maybe there was an element of pride in him when he had stood before that lion—a mixed motive. And that was why God had struck him down.

I saw it differently. The boy wasn't stupid. He just put his trust in a great Spirit that he couldn't see, and he believed that that Spirit was going before him and clearing his path and keeping him safe. It made sense that he believed that. He had been seduced by a wonderful story, a story that had been told so many times that it seemed it must be true. It was a story that I desperately wanted to believe—that people had more power than they could possibly imagine, that they were emissaries of the Lord. They simply needed to open their hearts and believe and then keep themselves pure, and then they could do anything in the world. Move mountains. Raise the dead. Call out to the lion in the name of the Lord and tell him to obey. That boy had believed the story with all of his heart, but he turned out to be wrong about God, wrong in the same way I had been.

〽️

A few days later, Yemi's friend Ruth, whom I'd first met in Akwa Ibom, dropped by my room to check up on me. She and I had been supposed to speak together on a panel on child witchcraft accusations that Yemi had organized and then suddenly canceled in the wake of the accident. She hadn't heard the reason, though, and she cried out when I opened the door and unveiled my black eye and the bandage that covered the bloody row of stitches on my left ear. I moved my drying clothes from the one chair in my dorm room and perched on the bed next to her, telling her about the accident.

Thank God, she kept murmuring, again and again, as I told her how bad it could have been. We traded gossip about mutual friends and I asked about the children at Sam's center. When the conversation began losing steam she seemed agitated, and I sensed there was something she wasn't saying. Finally, she lifted her hands from her lap, where they were busy twisting up the handles of the bag she was carrying, and that's when she asked me if I was a Christian.

Never before in my life had I answered that question honestly. If it was Yemi or Hannah doing the asking, I said no too quickly, almost defensively, shrugging the question away. If it was a pastor or one of the Christians I was interviewing, I dissembled, trying to avoid a direct answer. But this time, I told the truth. I carefully considered the question, looked Ruth in the eye, and told her no. I wasn't a Christian anymore.

Ruth started, and I didn't know how to explain myself. I had nothing at all against Jesus. I actually admired him—he was radical in every way, turning over the money changers' tables, breaking one rule after another, speaking in strange stories and parables. If I had lived in the same time as he did, I might have given away all of my things and followed him. If I had managed to find a church that truly followed his teachings, I might have joined up with them. Or maybe not. I'd already proven myself to be unwilling—or incapable—of following the doctrine of purity and abstinence that was so intrinsic to my childhood faith. But I didn't say any of that to Ruth. I just told her that I admired Jesus very much, and then let my apostasy sit heavily in the thick, humid air.

And then Ruth asked me if I believed in the Bible. Small beads of sweat bloomed on my brow. I said that parts of the Bible were probably true, and even the parts that weren't true were important stories, stories that had something to teach us. She shook her head sadly, and one of her braids fell away from the others. She brushed it away from her face. "They are not just stories," she said, her voice hardening. She began a campaign for my soul, and my blood rose a bit. To her vivid protestations I just shook my head sadly and said that there was a time when I believed very strongly, but that time had passed. When she asked me why, I couldn't tell her. I didn't know myself.

In a less tired, beaten-down mood I could have probably rallied a better explanation. I could have spoken of the ways that the church deviated from the teachings of Christ, the evidence scholars have given that much of the Bible is cobbled together. But instead I felt a surge of anger. I thought about the scars I had seen on children in the Niger Delta, inflicted by supposed men of God. I thought about the tremendous wealth the megachurches accumulated, at the expense of their impoverished parishioners. I thought of men and women all over the world who had been told from the pulpit that they were evil and broken because of who they desired.

And then I thought of the many hours I'd spent as a child scouring my Precious Moments Bible for God's promises and underlined them in pink and purple ink. The sick would be healed; the dead would rise up. No longer would there be weeping or gnashing of teeth. The lion would lie down with the lamb, and God would wipe every tear away. Once God finally had his way in the world, there would be nothing left to worry about. We'd be back in the garden again, together with God and with our families, safe forever from any force that would aim to harm us or destroy us. Safe from death. I wanted to look Ruth in the eye and tell her I didn't believe those promises anymore. But instead I spoke in fragments, and we both looked at the floor.

Ruth finally looked at her watch and said she'd better go. I didn't protest, just mumbled something about how I needed to do my work and bathe before it grew dark. I knew she thought me hard-hearted. That was the term I had also learned for those who, when confronted with the majesties of a wonder-working God, guard their hearts against them and continue in their immoral ways. When I closed the door behind her, I knew the conversation would probably send her to her knees in my honor later tonight, and maybe in the morning as well. And yet there was nothing I could say to appease her.

❦

I felt a headache start to rise up from the base of my skull, and with it a memory floated into my mind. A splash of stark afternoon sunlight against a bright pink wall—the basement bedroom of a friend of mine from high school. We were both gangly freshmen and we'd found each other on the fringes of our social circle. A few times a week her mom drove us back to her house and we watched MTV and ate chocolate-chip cookies. I was in the final burst of my devotion then—it would be two more years until I walked away from the church. I saw myself sitting on her bed, wide-eyed and earnest, proudly telling her about the way that we had all come together and built a church. She asked me what kind of church it was and I answered the way my mother would have. It was spirit-filled. She looked befuddled, and I explained that it was different from the run-of-the-mill churches you saw around the county—Methodist, Baptist, etc. We spoke directly to the Lord and he spoke to us. She kept looking at me oddly, and I realized that she and her family probably attended one of those churches, the ones that Pastor Jim said were dead.

"What do you believe?" I asked her. But she still looked bewildered.

"I don't believe in anything," she said.

She might as well have told me that she believed in unicorns or fairies. I was stunned, speechless. I found myself looking around her room, at her toys and clothes. Her parents were solidly middle class. Her father commuted to Washington, DC, every day in a suit and tie and her mother was a teacher. She had a three-piece bedroom set, bought new from Sears, a bookshelf full of colorful, brand-new paperbacks, her own stereo and television with a VCR attached, and a bean bag chair. I decided that those worldly goods must have tempted her away from the Lord. She was like the rich young man in the Book of Matthew, the one who approached Jesus and asked him what good deed he needed to do in order to have eternal life. Jesus chided him, telling him that he could only be saved if he kept himself pure, obeying the Ten Commandments. When the young man said he had already done that, Jesus told him that he needed to sell his possessions and give them to the poor. But the young man wasn't willing to do that. I assumed that my friend was the same way. It was no wonder that she didn't believe, when she had all these things to distract her away from God. And now Ruth probably thought that same thing about me.

※

Every day I walked to the clinic to have my stitches removed, but I always seemed to arrive when the procedure was impossible. Either the electricity was off or the undergraduates or pensioners had shut down the main gate to protest something the administration had done, and none of the doctors had been able to get through. After delaying the removal of the stitches several times, a resourceful nurse finally agreed to hold a flashlight while her colleague snipped at my stitches near a bright window. With my bandage finally off and my bruises fading, I felt freer to move around. I ventured out of my room to deliver gifts and say goodbye to professors, students, and friends who had been an integral part of my life in Nigeria. I sorted through my possessions and gave away clothing and books to make room for the heaps of photocopied papers that would be returning with me to the United States. Rather than visiting the cafeteria and retrieving a plate of plantains, rice, and fish to eat in my room, I fetched a plate and nestled into a sofa in the open-air foyer of the dormitory. This had been a habit before my accident, as some of the porters who guarded the entryway were always willing to loan out their copies of *Vanguard* or *The Nation*, Nigeria's tabloid-style daily newspapers.

This time, when I asked Mr. Abu for the paper, he shook his head while handing it to me.

"Bad happenings," he said, looking at me intently.

I stood at the edge of the registration counter and skimmed the front page of the paper. "Black Sunday in Lagos," the headline read. "Scores Burnt to Death as 21 Vehicles Crash." A color photo took up most of the front page: a mangled pile of charred cars and trucks, surrounded by hundreds of people. Men in shorts and soccer jerseys climbed the pile and pried at the metal, as if they were looking for survivors. But it was clear there weren't any survivors. I found myself searching the newspaper for numbers. They all conflicted. One bystander claimed that sixty people had died. A policeman said it had been twenty. Someone else said forty. There was no way to know for certain.

Mr. Abu explained what had happened. A checkpoint had been operating the day before, a Sunday, on the Lagos-Ibadan expressway, just south of Redemption Camp. A long line of cars, trucks, and *danfos* had been idling at a police checkpoint near the Shangisa Bridge on the outskirts of Lagos, waiting for their turn to flash their papers and naira in the direction of a police officer. The official story was that the brakes on a semi-truck hauling petrol from the north failed just in advance of the line of cars. But others said that the policemen started chasing the truck in an effort to extort money from the driver, and then the truck lost control and plowed into a long line of cars, igniting an explosion and starting a massive fire. Mr. Abu shook his head. He said that most of the people who died had just left the Redeemed Church's convention service. They were still wearing their Sunday clothes.

My hands trembled as I listened to Mr. Abu's account of the accident and stared at the graphic pictures in the newspaper. I told him how I had originally planned to go to the Redeemed Church's annual convention, and if I had stuck to my original schedule, I would have been heading south to Lagos around the same time as this car accident. Mr. Abu recoiled as if stung.

"Praise God," he whispered. "He kept you safe. You had your other accident to stop you from that."

My heart flared up in my chest, and for a moment I felt myself leaping back into the world of magical thinking, the universe as a series of divine interventions. *There but for the grace of God.* Maybe God was protecting me after all. Perhaps I had been spared. But if God had maneuvered events in such a way that my previous accident had kept me alive, why didn't he do as much for those who had died? I abandoned my plate of plantains and studied the rest of the article. One eyewitness managed to escape from a bus and watched eighteen of his fellow passengers, including his brother, as they burned alive. Another man and his wife got out of their car as soon as they heard the explosion, then leapt away as the flames spread to their own car. That man said, "We would have been like one of these ones, if not for God."

❧

I climbed the stairs to my dormitory room and began packing my things. All my notebooks and papers. The careful lists I'd made of all my expenses. The ultraviolet water purifier that I'd bought from that Scottish nurse back in Houston and never used once. The gifts I'd gotten for my family—strong-smelling red leather wallets and heavy

black-and-white beads. Endless piles of books that I'd purchased at university bookstores and market stalls. The fabric
I'd bought for two hundred naira a yard at the fabric markets
in Kano. My new Bible. My digital camera and the memory cards, full of photographs. I gathered up my kerosene
stove and pillow and the buckets I'd used to haul water, as
well as some leftover rice and pasta, and distributed them to
the graduate students on the hall. A few days later, when I
drove to the airport in Lagos, my driver caught my eye in the
rearview mirror and pointed out the black scar left on the
asphalt from the accident, just beyond the gates of Redemption Camp. I nodded and looked away and we drove the rest
of the way in silence.

Chapter 18

Back Home

Back in Houston over the next several years I developed a new kind of nervous tic. Whenever I felt anxious, my hand crept up to my cheek and found a scar on my cheekbone, no bigger than a fingernail, in the shape of a cross-stitch. When I brushed my fingers over it I could feel the grit that lay just under the surface—a minuscule shard of glass or fleck of gravel. When I first came back to Houston, a doctor had suggested surgery to cover it up, but I could barely afford the doctor's co-pay on my graduate-student salary. I guess I also thought the scar would fade with time, but I was wrong. That scar stayed with me as the years passed and my life took on a different shape. I graduated and took a job at a nonprofit, trading my faded corduroys and sneakers for button-down shirts and heels. I spent most of my days in a windowless room, patiently thumping meaning onto a pixelated screen with a set of plastic keys and springs, shuffling text around for hours at a time.

I stopped smoking cigarettes. I still filched them from friends out at bars and occasionally begged one from a stranger. But I gave up the daily habit, though the desire stayed with me. Any given evening after dinner I wanted nothing more than to get up from my couch, walk through my backdoor to the bodega on the corner of Richmond and Dunlavy, and ask the crotchety old man behind the counter for a pack of Camel Lights. I knew just how it would go. I'd walk back home with a spring in my step, a kind of adolescent impatience. I'd tear the plastic off the pack on my back stoop and then nab the lighter that my neighbor kept on top of the fuse box, just under the awning. I'd take one of those perfect cylinders from the box and put it to my lips, then light it and breathe in all that smoke and fire. I'd exhale and stare dreamily at the back fence, and then my ears would start to open up to all the noise of the world, engines firing and wind blowing through the live oaks, the footfalls on the sidewalk of a waiter with a clean white button-down on a hanger in his hand, on his way to work. I'd sink into all that noise and patter and then I'd come up clean. The thorny problems that had been tormenting me would recede as if they were called back to the sea, and I'd be left with a clear answer to some previously intractable problem. The rest of the cigarette would be smoked by a different kind of woman, a woman with a plan.

And yet I stayed home. I knew that the clarity provided by the nicotine would be short-lived, and after the first drag or two the cigarette would taste like ashes. Whenever that urge came upon me, I just drank another glass of water and reminded myself I'd finally built the life I wanted for myself, a life that felt like home. Instead of smoking I took up running. In the late afternoon at work, I'd shut my laptop, arch my back into a stretch, then slip into the bathroom to change into my running clothes. I'd drive a few miles to the trails in Memorial Park, the one wild place I'd found in

Houston, full of towering pines and live oaks. The forest was still broken from a long-ago hurricane, so it was a jungle of tree limbs and stumps, the leaves glimmering with humidity and vibrating with mosquitos. I lost myself in those trails for an hour or more, until the world of grammar and deadlines fell away and my brain finally stopped thinking in English and started turning to colors and shapes instead.

In the months after I left Nigeria, I sent Yemi a stack of GRE books he'd requested and wrote a long email to the sociology department at the University of Houston on his behalf, but nothing came of it. When the Afolabis visited their children an hour away from my home in Houston I drove up to see them. We sat for a while at the dining room table in their daughter's dark house, trading news back and forth. When they celebrated their fiftieth wedding anniversary a few years later, I sent a card at their daughter's request. Sam Itauma came to Houston once and we met in a chain restaurant and shared a blooming onion. I wrote a bit about my trip to the Niger Delta, but eventually the stacks of notebooks from my time in Nigeria ended up deep in the garage, buried under boxes of camping equipment and winter clothes.

Meanwhile on the other side of the world, everything kept on going as before. At Redemption Camp, Pastor Adeboye preached and thousands were saved, in Akwa Ibom the pump jacks kept tipping up and down, day and night, and oil kept on trickling between the roots of the mangroves. The pastors held court in the deliverance houses, Nkoyo shared a single bunk with three small girls, and Sam wrote pleas to funders in hopes of keeping the bags of rice coming. The policemen stopped *okadas*, demanding bribes of twenty naira to pass and threatening to shoot if the drivers tried to overrun them. Back in Ibadan Yemi taught philosophy to undergraduates. Meanwhile Helen Ukpabio preached another sermon in an open-air sanctuary in Cross River State. She claimed that she delivered a thousand witches without touching a single one.

Some people will argue that the farthest reaches of the world are closer than ever before, now that the continents are connected by an invisible web of satellites. But I don't find that to be true. Distance still erases everything. Over time you find yourself focusing on what's in front of you, despite your best intentions. The people you left behind move through the world without you. They may as well be gone. I thought of Jesus's disciples, who loved more deeply and more faithfully than I ever could. They had walked away from everything they had known to follow the man they believed to be the Messiah, and when the Romans arrested Jesus and nailed him to the cross, the disciples were devastated. They had lost their story, lost their reason for living. One scholar called them "a shattered group of defeated fugitives." But then they grieved so hard in that upper room that they brought the Spirit back with the force of their belief. Flickering orange flames appeared just above their heads, and suddenly they had the ability to pray in strange tongues. They bounded out of the house like men on fire, and when the crowds came, drawn by the noise and the spectacle, they were astonished to hear the miracles of God being spoken in their own language. Some in the crowd mocked them, saying they were drunk.

But then Peter stepped forward, reminding them of the prophecy that Joel had given centuries before. God had promised that in the last days, he would pour his Spirit out into the world. Sons and daughters would prophesy, young men would see visions, and old men would dream dreams. There would be wonders in heaven and signs on earth. The sun would turn to darkness and the moon to blood. On that day, whosoever called on the name of the Lord would be saved. Peter's words moved the crowd, and they begged him to tell them how they too could be saved. He told them to repent and be baptized, and then they would receive the gift as well.

Three thousand obeyed Peter's command and repented of their sins, and with that a new church was born. The disciples traveled two by two to far-off cities, telling of the good news and urging people to repent and be saved before it was too late. From the grief and despair of the twelve people who loved Jesus the most, a new faith was born. They were the ones who truly created Christianity, not Jesus himself. In his absence, their faith hardened and congealed like scar tissue. They weren't willing to let him go, to have the great promise of their belief in him vanish into nothing. So they kept telling the story that Jesus had seeded within them. A story with good news at the heart of it—that death is not the end, that there is something greater than death, greater than absence. That there is no such thing as the abyss, that the idea of losing each other is just a fever dream. When we die, we'll reunite in heaven with those we love, unless we stop following that book of rules and move outside of the circle.

❧

On a visit home three years later, I sat at the end of my mother's threadbare couch. My brother Joshua had stretched himself out on the other end of the couch, his socked feet nestled against my knee despite my protestations. He was eating vanilla ice cream with a grapefruit spoon. It had a serrated edge that he ran against his teeth after every bite.

Joshua was almost twenty-one now. He wore his hair longer than Obere and Sam ever had, and he was tall enough to duck when he climbed the stairs in my parents' house that led to his tiny upstairs bedroom. He was in college now at the University of Maryland, and when I asked him questions about his classes, he answered somewhat wearily. School was going fine. He was studying marketing and sometimes it was interesting, though most of the time the professors seemed to dial it in. He and his girlfriend were still dating, but his pastor didn't like them spending too much time together away from church. Yes, he was still going to the same church that my mother had told me about, the one with the Nigerian pastor. Abiding Word Family Christian Center.

I could hear him struggling to describe how he felt about the church. He must have known that I didn't believe anymore. But he couldn't quite help himself as he gushed about the community he'd found. As he talked I began to see how much it had overtaken his life. On Sundays he arrived at six in the morning to open up the church. After the morning service they hosted a potluck lunch, and then there was no point driving all the way home since the evening service started a few hours later. Wednesday was Bible study night and on Friday the night vigil started at 10 p.m. and sometimes lasted until one or two in the morning. Every other Saturday, Pastor Peter taught a special class for people who wanted to go into leadership, as my brother did, and on the intervening nights and weekends there was plenty to be done at the church. They had just moved into a new space—a former crab house—and Joshua was leading the renovation effort. As he talked I had to admit that he was glowing. He seemed deeply, almost disturbingly content when he talked about the church.

"I don't know how to put it," he said. "I just feel such a sense of peace. All of those things that I wanted at some point—buy a car, travel, get some important job—I don't want them anymore. I just want to help people and do God's work."

He stopped when he saw the look on my face. "I know it sounds crazy," he said. "I feel like I could get a job, I could finish college, but part of me says, why bother? I feel so peaceful, like those things have happened to me already."

I made a face and he smiled. "It must be hard to understand," he said. "Maybe you have to see it for yourself."

By that point I had attended hundreds of church services. What was one more? So the next morning I shook the wrinkles out of a sundress and borrowed a cardigan from my mother. She agreed to join me and the two of us made the long drive north to Accokeek. When we arrived at the church, there was a Hummer in the parking lot. My mother rolled her eyes and said it belonged to the pastor.

Joshua met us in the foyer wearing a sleek, well-tailored suit and ushered us into the sanctuary, a low-ceilinged room crowded with people. We were the only white attendees, but that didn't surprise me. Joshua's girlfriend had saved seats for us, and as we settled in, the pastor waved to us from the stage. He was a middle-aged Nigerian man with a widow's peak and a small, tight smile.

In the bulletin was a list of upcoming events. The dial-in number and conference line for a morning prayer call, every morning from 5 to 6 a.m. Announcements about marriage classes for newly engaged couples, A New Year's Eve celebration service, an all-night vigil on the first Friday of every month, an all-day "Word Service" on the third Saturday of each month. The profession of faith that was printed in the bulletin declared that this was a place where lives were changed, yokes were destroyed, and burdens were removed, and then prophesied that the church would become "the wealthiest, most anointed, and fastest growing ministry in the world." But once the worship service started, it didn't seem that different from any of the others I'd attended in the US or Nigeria. There were some hymns, newer ones that I didn't quite recognize, and then at the appropriate time people started lifting their hands to the Lord. I bowed my head politely and thought of other things until that part of the service was over.

When Pastor Peter began preaching, though, it was harder to distract myself. The sermon revolved around the idea of perfection. Pastor Peter argued that perfect physical health was within our reach. Christians had the blessing of God upon them, and that meant they could triumph over sickness and death, if only they believed. And of course, the way to demonstrate their faith was to give to the Lord. Pastor Peter promised the congregation that every cent they pledged to the Lord would come back to them tenfold in the coming months.

During the service Joshua stayed at the back of the sanctuary, whispering to the audio-visual guy about the sound. But when Pastor Peter wrapped up the sermon and served communion, Joshua stood next to him holding a silver tray of bread. When the rest of the congregation filed up to receive the body of Christ and drink his blood, I stayed in my seat.

I was sneaking a look at my phone when Pastor Peter called all the visitors up to the altar for prayer and healing. Two or three others stepped up to the front, and then Pastor

Peter called the rest of the congregation up to pray for them. After a moment it became clear that my mother and I were the only ones still sitting in our chairs. Pastor Peter began praising the Lord for meeting all our needs, making us whole, giving us the power to overcome the enemy.

I was still sitting in my seat next to my mother, playing through my day in my mind. By the time we got back to my parents' house, Sam would probably be there. My mother was going to make lasagna, and I'd drink a beer in the kitchen and help her chop onions. If my nephew took a nap and my father was in a good mood, then maybe we'd all play canasta.

That was when the pastor opened his eyes and interrupted his prayer. I heard my name and my spine went cold. I looked up and Pastor Peter was beckoning me to the front of the sanctuary. The people gathered there turned around to see who he was calling out to.

I smiled in a ridiculous way and shook my head slowly, and then the pastor's tone changed.

"Come here!" he said.

I shook my head again and my smile faded. My brother and his girlfriend were up there at the altar, and I wouldn't let myself look at them. I could tell that the pastor wasn't used to being disobeyed, and suddenly I was afraid. I stuttered out the word no, but it was too quiet.

Pastor Peter beckoned me again, his voice stern. He demanded some additional response, but my mind had gone soft. I couldn't think of what to say. Then the pastor rushed down the aisle in long strides, carrying his microphone with him.

"What do you believe?" he thundered. "Do you believe Jesus is the son of God?"

Tears welled up in my eyes and my neck turned beet red. I tried to talk but could only stammer. In that moment I became a child again, struck dumb in the face of a powerful man of God.

"I don't want—I don't believe . . ."

"It's a simple question," he snapped, looming over me.

In a quivering voice, I said, "I don't believe the same way that you do."

Suddenly my mother was standing up, putting herself between me and the pastor. She shouted at him, telling him to leave me alone. I'd never seen her so angry, had never heard her raise her voice like that in a public place. Meanwhile I remained in my seat, totally silent, tears running down my face.

The pastor shrank back, as surprised as I was by my mother's sudden outburst. He mumbled something about wanting to see me in his office after the sermon and then launched into one last prayer. My mother rummaged in her purse and pulled out a pack of tissues, and I tried to collect myself. As soon as the final prayer came to a close, I walked out of the sanctuary and stood in the foyer, shaking and catching my breath. The pastor's wife and daughter came over to me and held their hands out for a greeting. Joshua's girlfriend came over to me, and I could tell that she was embarrassed by what had happened. She said that when she first came to the church, she was surprised by the pastor's style. It didn't seem normal.

"It didn't seem normal because it's a cult," I snapped. My fear had evaporated and now I was furious, at the pastor for pressing me the way he did and at myself for not walking out right away. Joshua's girlfriend wouldn't meet my eyes.

On the long ride home, my mother bristled about how rude the pastor had been. She didn't mention my confession of doubt, or the fact that when we left the church, Joshua stayed behind. I didn't say much of anything. I was still humiliated, embarrassed that I had been so afraid of the pastor. What had kept me from slipping out of the sanctuary at the first sign that things were going wrong? Why had I not been able to defend myself? Why did I become a sniveling child when asked what I believed in? Why was I still so affected by the idea of renouncing the church, renouncing the Lord?

When we arrived home, my mother brushed aside the events of the morning and went to work in the kitchen. As she cooked, I stewed on the couch for hours, watching my nephew play with blocks and plotting how I would set Joshua straight. When he finally walked in, I attacked him immediately, telling him the pastor was a bully, and he was being brainwashed. But he just looked at me and then turned around and walked upstairs to his bedroom. I rushed outside and slammed the door, and then headed down the muddy hill that led to the beach.

I'd been taking that same walk for ten years, every time I flew to Maryland to visit my family. More often than not, Joshua would be beside me, picking wineberries from the bushes on the edge of the path, holding my arm when my sneakers slipped on the muddy clay, pointing out the trail that led to our neighbor's secret garden deep in the trees. He was five years old when my family first moved to the farm, and this landscape was the only one that he remembered. The beach that lay just beyond the stand of cattails was the same one where I'd first showed him how to find fossilized sharks' teeth, teaching him how to cement the blue-grey shape of a triangle in his mind and then let go of looking, raking his eyes across the pebbled beach until he saw that shape in the sand. Now he could find ten sharks' teeth for every one that I found.

Joshua was born when I was twelve. When I lived in Washington, after college, he'd come to visit for the weekend and we'd walk down the long hill of Sixteenth Street toward the museums, laughing at some of the paintings and standing quiet in front of others. Even then he was slightly suspicious about my choices, turning up his nose when I swore or ordered a beer. Even the group house I lived in went slightly against the grain. He couldn't get over the fact that none of us was in charge. I knew why this upset him. From an early age we had been drilled on a strict hierarchy: God was at the helm, and then the pastor, and then the head of the household, and then the mother, and then the children. He couldn't understand how my friends and I functioned without that kind of authority.

The landscape did its work on me and after an hour or so I climbed the steep hill up to the house, shivering from the cold. With every step I felt my anger coming back as I pictured the scene earlier that morning in church. But then I pried the squeaky screen door open and spotted my brother slumped onto the living room couch. His thick leather-bound Bible was open in his lap and he was taking notes in his block handwriting. From the kitchen, I could hear that my mother and father had started bickering. I found myself itching to get out of that cramped house and fly back to Houston, to turn the key in the lock and breathe in a house that smelled like me alone.

Joshua was almost twenty-one, but I realized that he had never felt that kind of freedom. He'd never lived away from home. Unlike me, he hadn't wanted to leave Maryland after high school. Instead, he'd taken classes at the local community college, so he could continue to live with my parents and work construction with my brother Sam, and then he'd transferred to the state university. To my knowledge he'd never sipped a beer or smoked a cigarette. Instead he devoted himself to purity, to living up to the vision that he felt God had for him. His faith was more important to him than anything else. I didn't like his pastor, but it wasn't right for me to judge my brother for what gave him comfort, blame him for what his pastor had done, or reject him simply because I rejected his faith. He deserved better, as I had at his age. So instead I just sat down next to him. When he looked up at me, I put my arm around him and rubbed his shoulders, the way I used to do back when we were kids.

❧

The years went on and time kept knocking against us, coarsening our skin and greying my parents' hair, turning us each into more of ourselves. Joshua graduated wearing a black gown with a red sash and a yellow scarf. My brothers followed in my father's entrepreneurial footsteps, starting their own businesses around the same time that my father stopped laying brick. My mother went back to school for social work and opened her own counseling practice. Jake and I decided to get married, and soon we were back in Maryland on Christmas Eve with an infant son of our own.

After we all ate dinner, my mother turned to me and asked if I'd join her for the Christmas Eve service. An old instinct had me about to say no, but then for some reason I shrugged and agreed to go with her. We tucked a fleece blanket around Silas and buckled him into his harness, and my mother drove slowly down that long dirt road in my father's rusted-out Ford. When Silas woke up and started squawking, my mother sang a fragment of a song over and over again, high and sweet. It was the same one she sang at my wedding. *As I went down to the river to pray, studying about that good old way, and who shall wear the robe and crown, good Lord show me the way.* My low voice joined hers. My mother always had perfect pitch, and next to hers my voice sounded better than it was. Our voices put the baby to sleep again and then the only sound left was the deep rumble of the diesel engine.

A few years earlier my mother had started going back to the same church that we grew up in, the one on the corner of Ball Road and Route 4. It wasn't called Rock Church anymore. It was Crossroads Church now, and Jim Cucuzza had been out of the pulpit for years. One of the girls I grew up with married one of those scrawny, pockmarked boys from our youth group and he was in the pulpit now. His sermons were long on love and compassion and light on deliverance, and under his leadership the church had become quieter, less demonstrative, more like those mainstream churches we once derided. The old sanctuary was a gymnasium now, and the stones my father laid behind the altar were gone, pried out maybe, or painted over. But some things hadn't changed. There on the corner of Ball Road and Route 4 was the same old nativity structure they'd been using for years, lopsided with fresh pine boughs on the roof. Some other family was dressed up in robes and costume jewelry, waving furiously at the cars below.

Most of the Christmas Eve service was made up of songs. The projector reminded us of the lyrics, but these were songs that all of us knew: "Away in a Manger," "Hark the Herald Angels Sing," "Silent Night." The children put on a Christmas play and a trio of small angels with pipe-cleaner halos danced around a plastic baby doll. One of the angels wore her mother's lipstick and was as confident as a child actress, while the other two moved stiffly and awkwardly, following her lead. At some point, an African American woman with short hair and a dark-red velvet dress sang a beautiful song with low orchestral accompaniment.

I found myself relaxing at some point in the service. Everything was quieter and dimmer than I remembered it being, and I didn't see anyone I recognized. Fifteen years had passed since we were regular members of that church, and now we were surrounded by strangers. Even so, I felt a strange sense of camaraderie with them. Each of the families that lined the pews had dressed up, tweezed and shaved and pulled on something scratchy, stuffed their children into coats and made their way out into the dark night, to come together for a greater purpose—to celebrate the birth of the God they worshipped.

At no point did the orchestra usher the congregation away from the hymns and toward a mystical world, and only a few people raised their hands when they sang. At no point did I hear someone or something condemned, or hear judgment in the pastor's voice. With my son sleeping next to me in his car seat, and my mother next to me in the chair, I felt safe. No one was going to call me to the stage or examine my credentials. But even if they did, I knew how I would answer.

Just before the service ended the ushers passed out the candles with little cardboard circles around their base, to protect our fingers from being burned. The pastor lit the flame from a large white pillar candle that sat on a stand near the altar, and then the ushers dipped their candles into that flame. The fire spread from person to person.

Silas began whimpering. I bent down and took him from the stroller and held him on my shoulder, cupping his head in my hand so he could take in the scene. He furrowed his wrinkled brow at all those wavering flames, wearing an overly serious look that he got from my husband. The sanctuary was a foreign world to him. He had never seen candles before, or preschool-aged angels with lopsided ponytails. He would never fall asleep during a long Sunday evening service, his head resting on his father's lap, a suit jacket covering him like a blanket. He'd probably never lie awake in his bed at night, mulling over the mystery of the Holy Trinity or puzzling over New Testament parables. He wouldn't know the heady power you gained from cleaving close to God and keeping his commandments. He'd probably never live his life in a state of siege, convinced that every earthly action has a heavenly consequence. Instead Silas would grow up as his father had, deeply involved in the things of this world, seeing compassion and kindness as values in their own right, rather than keys to the kingdom.

It would probably go the same way for me. My days of seeking were over. I'd never again lose myself in a worship service, my head bowed and hands lifted. I'd never summon up the courage to share the good news with a stranger. I'd never lay hands on my son and demand that the demons of sickness flee from his body, and I'd never again leave my earthly language behind and speak in the tongues of angels. If a prayer rose up in my throat in some moment of happiness or fear, I'd push it back down. But I would never stop missing the old days.

Back in my mother's kitchen, a splotched photograph dangled off the refrigerator from a greasy magnet. It was a black-and-white family portrait, taken by my father on the self-timer of his ancient Mamiya. In it he was looming to the rear of the family, glaring into the camera while my mother wore a tight, closed-lip smile. Obere and Sam were just kids, and Joshua wasn't born yet. Judging from my braces and tortoise-shell glasses, I was probably eleven or twelve. In the photograph we were all smooshed together, so close you can hardly see whose arms are whose. I had never been able to look at that picture without feeling the weight of everything I had lost. I knew there was no path back to the time when I believed in God with the innocence of a child. We weren't the same family anymore, and I wasn't the same girl who plunged herself into the blue-tinged chlorinated water of that baptismal font, pinching her nose and holding her breath, praying to be touched by the Spirit.

In the years to come Jake and Silas and I would keep making the long trek to Maryland, and new family pictures would start to crowd out that old snapshot. Silas's hair would come in blond and straight, just like that of his uncles, and my father would take his small hand in his and show him how to scatter grain for the guinea hens in their backyard coop. Maybe in a few years my brothers would take Silas down to the beach and teach him how to spot sharks' teeth in the litter of shells and stones on the shoreline. Perhaps my mother and I would get into the habit of going to Christmas Eve services together.

From his perch on my shoulder Silas mewed. He was getting hungry. I laid my hand on his back, watching as the family in the row in front of us carefully passed a flickering flame from one candle to another. Finally it was our turn. The white-haired woman to my mother's left caught the fire, and then walked a few slow steps toward my mother, protecting her flame with a wrinkled hand. My mother lit her candle, and then she passed the fire to me. I held the candle a safe distance from Silas, and he squinted at it, trying to figure out what that strange substance was. By the time I looked up and out over the sanctuary, every single person held a candle with the same orange and wavering flame. For a moment my vision blurred, and it looked as if we were all on fire.

Acknowledgments

Sincere thanks to the editors at publications in which portions of this book first appeared, including Jodee Stanley at *Ninth Letter*, Juliana Kruis at *Redivider*, Brianna Van Dyke at *Ruminate*, Brianne Carpenter at *Sycamore Review*, Desirae Matherly at the *Tusculum Review*, and Bill Henderson, who edits the Pushcart anthology.

Very special thanks to Amy Caldwell, my wonderful editor, and Matt McGowan, my incredibly supportive agent. Without their passion, support, and guidance, this book would not have been possible. I'm also grateful to the entire team at Beacon Press for their support, especially Helene Atwan, Susan Lumenello, Pamela MacColl, Molly Velázquez-Brown, and Perpetua Charles. Beacon Press is a national treasure, and I can't think of a better home for this book.

Thanks to everyone who read these pages in various forms and offered feedback, including Martha Serpas, Alexander Parsons, Nick Flynn, j. Kastely, Antonya Nelson, Robert Boswell, Mat Johnson, Briana Olson, Jason Bruner, Nathan Suhr-Sytsma, and Tom Huang. Special thanks to Kimberly Meyer, whose encouragement over the past nine years has meant everything to me. I'm also grateful to Leslie Leyland Fields, Lia Purpura, Leslie Jamison, and Steven Church for seeing the potential in my work and selecting early material for various prizes.

Thanks to the University of Houston, Inprint, the Houston Arts Alliance, the Virginia Center for the Creative Arts, the Wild Acres residency program, and the West Africa Research Association, which made it possible for me to travel to Nigeria in the summer of 2010.

Thanks to everyone who supported my research, including Hosam Aboul-Ela, Gary Foxcroft, Tony Fadele, James Fadele, J. D. Y. Peel, Elias Bongmba, Kairn Klieman, Sam Itauma, Adeyemi Johnson Ademowo, Matthews Ojo, Leo Igwe, Ademola Omobewaji Dasylva, Isaac Ayegboyin, and Toyin Jegede.

I'm also grateful to the many friends who gave me the courage to claim my story, especially Sasha Pitrof, Jennifer Meridian, Michelle Mariano, Aja Gabel, Rhianna Tyson Kreger, Ayleen Pérez Cordeiro, Kenya Bradshaw, Corey Noll, Christine Ha, Thea Lim, and Claire Anderson.

Very special thanks to my husband, Jacob Reimer, my first and best reader, and my son, Silas, who has brought so much joy to my life.

Most of all, thanks to my beloved family: Bo, Anne, Obere, Sam, and Joshua Wilbanks.

A Note on Sources

The early story of Rock Church is captured in the book *Upon This Rock: The Remarkable Story of John and Anne Gimenez* as told to Robert Paul Lamb (Virginia Beach, VA: Souls Books, 1983). For the history of Pentecostalism in the United States, I depended heavily on a number of books and articles by scholars of religion, including Allan Anderson's *Introduction to Pentecostalism: Global Charismatic Christianity* (Cambridge, UK: Cambridge University Press, 2004); Robert M. Anderson's *Visions of the Disinherited: The Making of American Pentecostalism* (Peabody, MA: Hendrickson Publishers, 1979); Harvey Cox's *Fire from Heaven: The Rise of Pentecostal Spirituality and the Reshaping of Religion in the Twenty-First Century* (Cambridge, MA: Da Capo Press, 2001); Mark Galli's 1995 piece "Revival at Cane Ridge" from *Christianity Today*; Gary McGee's *Miracles, Missions, and American Pentecostalism* (Maryknoll, NY: Orbis Books 2010); Robert Owens's *The Azusa Street Revival: Its Roots and Its Message* (Lanham, MD: University Press of America, 1998); Grant Wacker's *Heaven Below: Early Pentecostals and American Culture* (Cambridge, MA: Harvard University Press, 2001); an 1895 article from the *Atlanta Journal Constitution* entitled "Wonderful If True: How an Ignorant Negro Girl Acquired the Gift of Tongues"; and research from the Center for Religion and Civic Culture's Pentecostal and

Charismatic Research Initiative, housed at the University of Southern California 2009–13.

Particularly helpful sources on the rise of Pentecostalism in the global south included the Pew Research Center's 2006 report *Spirit and Power: A Ten-Country Survey of Pentecostals*; Paul Gifford's *African Christianity: Its Public Role* (Bloomington: Indiana University Press, 1998); Donald E. Miller and Tetsunao Yamamori's *Global Pentecostalism: The New Face of Christian Social Engagement* (Berkeley: University of California Press, 2007); Moses Olatunde Oladeji's *Understanding the Pentecostal Movement* (Ibadan, Nigeria: Bounty Press, 2005); Matthews Ojo's "American Pentecostalism and the Growth of Pentecostal-Charismatic Movements in Nigeria," from *Freedom's Distant Shores: American Protestants and Post-Colonial Alliances with Africa*, edited by R. Drew Smith (Waco, TX: Baylor University Press, 2006); Iain MacRobert's *The Black Roots and White Racism of Early Pentecostalism in the USA* (New York: St. Martin's Press, 1988); and two books by Ogbu Kalu: *African Pentecostalism: An Introduction* (Oxford, UK: Oxford University Press, 2008) and *The History of Christianity in West Africa* (London: Longman, 1980).

Reporters at the *Dallas Morning News* have covered Redemption Camp extensively. I drew on Scott Farwell's 2005 article "African Church Plans 'Christian Disneyland'" and his 2008 article "Nigerian Church Brings Noise, Passion to Small Texas Town," as well as on Tegan Hanlon's 2013 article "Redeemed Christian Church of God Dedicates $15.5 Million Pavilion Center." Simon Romero's 2005 article in the *New York Times*, "A Texas Town Nervously Awaits a New Neighbor," was also helpful, as were Brenda Huey's book *The Blackest Land, the Whitest People: Greenville, Texas*

(Bloomington, IN: AuthorHouse, 2006); Jason Margolis's 2014 *BBC News* piece "The Redeemed Church of God Preaches the Gospel in the US"; Andrew Rice's 2009 piece in the *New York Times Magazine*, "Mission from Africa"; and W. Walworth Harrison's *History of Greenville and Hunt County, Texas* (Waco, TX: Texian Press, 1976). I also drew on a 2003 article by Laolu Akande on the Celestial Church of Christ website, "Redeemed Christian Church of God Buys Multi-Million Dollar Property Near Dallas."

Details about Enoch Adeboye come from several sources, including an official biography that I purchased at Redemption Camp in Nigeria, Rebecca Bible-Davids's *Enoch Adeboye: Father of Nations* (Charlotte, NC: Biblos Publishers, 2009); Asonzeh Ukah's *A New Paradigm of Pentecostal Power: A Study of the Redeemed Christian Church of God in Nigeria* (Trenton, NJ: Africa World Press, 2008); and Lisa Miller's 2008 profile of Adeboye in *Newsweek* were helpful as well.

The quote about how to identify a child witch is from Helen Ukpabio's *Unveiling the Mysteries of Witchcraft* (Calabar, Nigeria: Liberty Foundation Gospel Ministries, 1996), a digest of witchcraft activities vividly illustrated with examples from her own ministry. I also viewed her 1999 film *End of the Wicked*, directed by Teco Benson. Additional sources included Mark Oppenheimer's 2010 *New York Times* article "On a Visit to the U.S., a Nigerian Witch-Hunter Explains Herself" and Daniel Offiong's *Witchcraft, Sorcery, Magic, and Social Order Among the Ibibio of Nigeria* (Enugu, Nigeria: Fourth Dimension Publishing, 1991).

I am grateful to many sources for a deeper understanding of Yorùbá culture, colonialism, and the history of Nigeria, including but not limited to J. F. Ade Ajayi's *Christian Missions* in Nigeria, 1841–1891: The Making of a New Élite (Chicago: Northwestern University Press, 1969); Emmanuel Ayank-anmi Ayandele's *The Missionary Impact on Modern Nigeria, 1842–1914: A Political and Social Analysis* (London: Long-mans, 1966); Robin Horton's *Patterns of Thought in Africa and the West: Essays on Magic, Religion, and Science* (Cambridge, UK: Cambridge University Press, 1993); J. D. Y. Peel's *Religious Encounter and the Making of the Yoruba* (Blooming-ton: Indiana University Press, 2003); the *Journals of the Rev. James Frederick Schön and Mr. Samuel Crowther* (London: Cass, 1970); Wole Soyinka's *Myth, Literature, and the African World* (Cambridge, UK: Cambridge University Press, 1976); and Ngũgĩ wa Thiong'o's *Decolonising the Mind: The Politics of Language in African Literature* (London: James Currey, 1986). I am particularly grateful to Ayodeji Abodunde, an inde-pendent researcher based in Ibadan, for his comprehensive book *A Heritage of Faith: A History of Christianity in Nigeria* (Ibadan, Nigeria: Pierce Watershed, 2009).

Additional sources include Jude Isiguzo's 2010 article in the *Nation*, "Black Sunday in Lagos," Leo Bawa's book *Nations in Agony* (Abuja, Nigeria: Still Waters Publications, 2002), and G. Elijah Dunn's book *Leaving Fundamentalism: Personal Sto-ries* (Ontario: Wilfrid Laurier University Press, 2008).